THE ALL-NEW

FREE TO BE THIN

BOOKS BY NEVA COYLE

Abiding Study Guide
Daily Thoughts on Living Free
Diligence Study Guide
Discipline Study Guide
Discipline tape album (4 cassettes) with guide
Free to Be Thin, The All-New (with Marie Chapian)
Free to Be Thin Lifestyle Plan, The All-New
Free to Be Thin Cookbook
Free to Be Thin Daily Planner
Free to Dream
Freedom Study Guide
Getting Your Family on Your Side (with David Dixon)
Learning to Know God
Living Free
Living Free Seminar Study Guide
Making Sense of Pain and Struggle
Meeting the Challenges of Change
A New Heart . . . A New Start
Obedience Study Guide
Overcoming the Dieting Dilemma
Perseverance Study Guide
Restoration Study Guide
Slimming Down and Growing Up (with Marie Chapian)
There's More to Being Thin Than Being Thin (with Marie Chapian)

BOOKS BY MARIE CHAPIAN

Am I the Only One Here With Faded Genes?
Discovering Joy
Feeling Small Walking Tall
Free to Be Thin, The All-New (with Neva Coyle)
Help Me Remember, Help Me Forget
Making His Heart Glad
Mothers and Daughters
His Gifts to Me
His Thoughts Toward Me
Of Whom the World Was Not Worthy
Secret Place of Strength
Slimming Down and Growing up (with Neva Coyle)
Telling Yourself the Truth (with William Backus)
There's More to Being Thin Than Being Thin (with Neva Coyle)
Why Do I Do What I Don't Want to Do? (with William Backus)

NEVA COYLE·MARIE CHAPIAN

THE ALL-NEW FREE TO BE THIN

BETHANY HOUSE PUBLISHERS
MINNEAPOLIS, MINNESOTA 55438
A Ministry of Bethany Fellowship, Inc.

Published by Bethany House Publishers
A Ministry of Bethany Fellowship, Inc.
11300 Hampshire Avenue South
Minneapolis, Minnesota 55438

Printed in the United States of America

Library of Congress Cataloging-in-Publication Data

Coyle, Neva, 1943–
    The all-new free to be thin / Neva Coyle, Marie Chapian.
      p. cm.
Rev. ed. of: Free to be thin / Marie Chapian
    1. Reducing—Religious aspects. 2. Christian life—1960–
I. Chapian, Marie. II. Chapian, Marie. Free to be thin. III. Title.
RM222.2.C44   1993
613.2'5—dc20   93–25600
ISBN 1–55661–312–1   Hardcover   CIP
ISBN 1–55661–534–5   Paperback.

To the
one million people
who have lost weight
on the
Free to Be Thin
program.

NEVA COYLE is Founder of Overeaters Victorious and President of Neva Coyle Ministries. Presently she is the Coordinator of Departmental Ministries in her church. Her ministry is enhanced by her bestselling books, tapes, as well as by her being a gifted motivational speaker/teacher. Neva and her husband make their home in California.

She may be contacted at:

P.O. Box 2330
Orange, CA 92669

MARIE CHAPIAN, Ph.D., is known around the world as an inspirational author and speaker. She also is a Christian counselor and a familiar personality to radio and TV audiences. Having authored more than 25 books, with translations in over two dozen languages, she has received many awards for her writing, including the Evangelical Christian Publishers Association Gold Medallion Award and the *Cornerstone* Book of the Year Award.

Contents

1

REALLY FREE TO BE THIN

Forget the former things; do not dwell on the past.
(Isaiah 43:18)

In the first edition of *Free to Be Thin* (published in the summer of 1979), we talked about a woman named Carolee who is the typical overweight overeater. When Carolee reached 90 pounds overweight, she felt miserable and desperate. Her health was deteriorating and so was her zest for life. She agonized at being overweight, suffered with multiple health problems, and was often depressed to the point of hopelessness. Although she agonized about her health and weight problems, she could not seem to get control over her eating. In fact, the worse she felt the more she seemed to lose control and to overeat and gorge on foods high in fat.

It was not that Carolee did not try. Far from it. Carolee went on dozens of diets. If she lost 10 pounds, she would gain back 20. If she lost 20 pounds, she gained back 30. Carolee was at a point of desperation when she turned to God for help. At the time we met her, she carried 210 pounds on her five-foot one-inch frame.

Carolee's experience parallels the lives of thousands of men and women who find themselves on a troubling cycle: They overeat and diet, overeat and diet—never able to attain that "mystical balance" that will keep them thin. *Thin!* That was all Carolee wanted. She had already tried everything she could think of. She had eaten the diet candy, chewed the diet gum, swallowed the diet pills. She'd joined the clubs, eaten nothing but shakes and salads, and her shelves were full of the many weight-loss books that are published every year. She'd even tried hypnosis and acupuncture. When she begged a surgeon for the painful and life-threatening bypass surgery, he told her she wasn't fat enough.

As I (Neva) can tell you, people are truly desperate when they pursue such a horrible and serious operation such as bypass surgery. It includes slicing across the stomach, making a 15- to 18-inch incision to disconnect approximately nine feet of the small intestines, leaving the patient with 18 inches of a functioning intestine. The agonizing side effects and complications are the price paid for a fleeting moment of so-called thinness.

Carolee talked with me shortly after I had started what was to become the phenomenally successful weight-loss program called *Overeaters Victorious.* I told Carolee about my own suffering with the bypass surgery. "I had a real problem. And whenever I face a problem that seems impossible, I *know* the answer has to be with God." Carolee seemed gripped by the words, and the following week she started on the "Free to Be Thin" program. Perhaps God would help her, too.

At the time Marie and I wrote the book *Free to Be Thin,* Carolee had already lost 70 pounds. The weight loss was not the prominent thing, though—there was a dramatic change inside her. Physically, emotionally, and spiritually, she was a new person. As we write this book, she is no longer a slave to her body and a victim of her eating habits. Today she continues to celebrate what God has done for her: "The real victory is what has happened in my life," she says. "I won a true victory over ignorance and self-indulgence." You see, as Carolee discovered, *life is what happens inside you, no matter what kind of physical state you are in*!

Thousands of *Free to Be Thin* readers have shared openly how God has helped them overcome anger, fear, jealousy, loneliness, frustration, and shame. Being healthier, stronger, and leaner is a dream come true—but even better is the fact that they are whole, new persons on the inside.

The Bible tells us "nothing is impossible with God" (Luke 1:37). That includes being free from overeating. The goal of *The All-New Free to Be Thin* lifestyle plan is to show you how to put overeating and food abuse in your past forever. You can be free from overeating, and you can *stay* free. We can offer that hope, not because we are offering new pills or "magic formulas," but because you are about to learn a new way of life.

Overeating and poor eating do not affect only the body. Your eating habits are intricately intertwined with your emotions. We know, for example, that the *way* we eat and *what* we eat directly represents our inner state. When we "stuff" and when we "dabble," we demonstrate different attitudes. When we lie listlessly on the couch wolfing down chocolate, we are giving a completely different emotional message than when we sit at the table dining on a healthy, savory meal. It is a fact that nearly any time an overeater's emotions go awry, he or she will reach for food. Authorities on obesity tell us that emotional tension is one of the triggers for the overeater to overeat—and it will actually *stimulate* the desire for food. Any food.

Gorging on food wounds more than our bodies. Our souls are hurt, too. Compulsive acts that are not driven by chemical imbalance or disease affect us in ways that undermine and destroy our self-confidence. In *The All-New Free to Be Thin* lifestyle plan, you will discover the joy of a changed life, because losing weight is more than finding the right diet. If you are really serious about changing your life, now is the time to start.

We have been making excuses for destroying our bodies far too long. The overeat-diet cycle is destructive. Bouncing back and forth, with one 10- to 20-pound-weight-loss experience after another, is far more harmful to your body than you realize.

The Lord Jesus Christ died on the cross so that His people no longer need to be the victims of self-destruction and suffering. We no longer need to be victims of compulsive acts. You may ask then, "Are my poor eating habits and overeating *sin*?" Many people do not consider poor eating habits to be sin. When nutritious and healthy food is available to you, can it be good stewardship of your God-created body to eat those foods that only cause you discomfort, unhappiness, and poor health?

"Wait a minute," you may resist. "My eating habits can't be sin. I'm free to be who I am as a Christian person, disciplined or undisciplined. The Lord loves me just the way I am. He loves me with all my faults and that's the way it is."

Let's take another look at overeating: One of the chief reasons for overeating and body abuse is that we don't really believe we are truly and totally loved. Food takes the role of the Comforter.

What shall we say then? Shall we go on sinning so that grace may increase? By no means! (Romans 6:1–2)

Yes, it is true that God loves you. And, like a loving parent, He wants to train you to hear and obey His voice so that you will be kept from harm and be able to live a full, rich, empowered, *happy* life.

There's the key to dynamic living and power: *obedience.* The Bible tells us in Galatians 5:23 that evidence of the Holy Spirit's working in our lives is self-control. Therefore, our goal in *The All-New Free to Be Thin* lifestyle plan is to help you learn how to hear the Lord and how to obey Him when He gently urges, "Don't eat that." Marie and I will share with you what we have learned and what we have seen take place in the lives of thousands of others as a result of allowing the Holy Spirit to take hold of the reins of our appetites.

Our first step, then, toward freedom and health is to consider the commitment before us. It's a wonderful and powerful commitment, one that will have a dynamic effect on us for the rest of our lives.

Take a deep breath, and get ready to begin.

2

MAKING A COMMITMENT

God longs to be the guiding force in your life, longs to fill *every* need you have—including the need to eat in a health-giving and non-destructive way.

Ask yourself this question: "Will I allow the Holy Spirit of God to teach me wise eating habits?"

If your answer is *yes,* you're ready to begin.

Let's begin with control. What is it? We know what *lack* of control is, but what do we mean when we say we've got control? One woman said, after being in a *Free to Be Thin* class only three weeks, "Self-control is like a great big hug. It wraps its arms around you and keeps you safe."

Making a commitment is the beginning. You're going to start training yourself with the help of the Holy Spirit. Don't be afraid. In the past you may have failed, but God is a patient and loving God. Maybe you have lost weight and gained it back and, in despair, you gave up choosing healthy foods. But the Lord is right beside you at this moment—ready to begin work with you on your eating habits.

WHAT KIND OF EATER ARE YOU?

Since *Free to Be Thin* was first published, we have observed and studied the types of eaters who tend to have problems with food. It is important to identify the type of eater you are in order to determine the changes you're going to make. If you are an *overweight overeater,* chances are that your out-of-control eating habits are the major contributor to your weight struggles. You only restrict your food intake with a goal weight in mind, then gradually lose your focus and overeat your way back to your formerly fat self. These patterns of self-destruction often begin early in adolescence and are troublesome most of a person's adult life. Overeating often includes poor eating. The second type of eater is the *overweight poor eater*. You will overeat *and* eat foods that are harmful to your body. Both of these types are not overweight due to muscle weight, such as the athlete may have. We are talking about *fat*.

The third type of eater is the *fluctuating-weight overeater*. This is the person who can lose weight and then maintain a reasonable, steady weight for a while—only to pop up another 10 or 20 pounds of fat seemingly overnight. The result is usually a return to an unhealthy mind-set and subsequent unhealthy eating. Most of us do not become unhealthy and miserable eating reasonable amounts if foods are natural, vitamin and mineral filled, fat-free, and wholesome.

The exception, of course, is the person who has real, bona-fide food allergies. Then it is important to adjust the diet. Many books and programs will advise eating foods that may not be good for *you*. One person may find whole wheat perfectly healthy; another, have an allergic reaction. Many people are allergic to corn and dairy products.

Throughout this book, we will be talking about the overweight overeater, the overweight poor eater, and the fluctuating-weight overeater. All three types are food abusers. Just as the drug abuser or the alcohol abuser is in need of more than abstinence by itself, so is the food abuser in need of more than a diet. To quit eating or drastically change your intake of food will not reach the root of the disorder.

When the food abuser chooses to destroy her or his body and completely disregard the basic rules of health and longevity, there's more involved than food. We need to take time to consider and understand the forces at work within the whole person.

A Great Big Hug

We are made of body, soul, and spirit. In order to be rightly aligned with the will of God, your *spirit* should be the controlling force in your life. Your human spirit, indwelt and empowered by the Holy Spirit, is then able to be in constant communion with God. It's a beautiful place to be. You are able to hear His voice, understand His Word, and obey Him daily. As your spirit aligns with God, your body and your soul respond to His power. He loves you so dearly and wants you to know His power and feel His love.

If your physical *appetite* tells your spirit what to do, you are living out of order. You have opened yourself to defeat. Likewise, if your soul is in control—and this is the area most people are led by—you are also living out of order. Your soul is comprised of intellect, emotion, and will. If your emotions lead your life, you are vulnerable to any circumstance or event. If your intellect alone guides your life, you are without the wisdom of God who is all wisdom. If your natural human will is directing your life, then you are, at best, as stubborn and inflexible as the rest of us when we have determined a goal for ourselves and do not know how to live in cooperation with God.

Sometimes selfishness becomes obvious. The person who says, for instance, "My overeating is not because of deep emotional needs. I eat because I enjoy food," could really be saying, "I don't want God to tamper with my appetite. I don't want to change. I don't want to face and deal with what is hurting me." That person may not like the idea of discipline or the godly fruit of self-control—but God's will is to free you from selfishness. And so He wants the arms of self-control to wrap around you in "a great big hug," keeping you safe.

THE ARGUMENT WITH GOD

You're going to make a deal now, an agreement. The Bible talks about the importance of a covenant, which is a *binding and solemn agreement.* Just before God gave Moses the tablets of the Law, He showed him the importance of a covenant—that is, a "binding and solemn agreement." The agreement was important in order to be successful, or to prosper. *Prosper* means to be successful, to thrive. Is it your goal to prosper in your efforts to change destructive overeating patterns?

God promises prosperity and success for keeping a covenant.

Carefully follow the terms of this covenant, so that you may prosper in everything you do. (Deuteronomy 29:9)

When you enter into this covenant, you make an agreement with God to eat His way. You know all too well that your own attempts to change without Him will bring you disappointment and failure. But God will not disappoint you. Be assured that He is joining *with* you. A covenant, or an agreement, takes more than one. God will not only encourage you on your way to freedom, He will also show you the way!

> *You are standing today in the presence of the Lord your God. . . . You are standing here in order to enter into a covenant with the Lord your God, a covenant the Lord is making with you this day and sealing with an oath, to confirm you this day as his people, that he may be your God as he promised you and as he swore to your fathers, Abraham, Isaac and Jacob.* (Deuteronomy 29:10, 12–13)

THE COMMITMENT

When you enter into a covenant with God you can expect results. You're a person who means business. You are agreeing *with* Him to go on a definite retraining program. When you come to God on His terms, seeking His way, asking His guidance, He will guide, comfort, encourage, strengthen, and see to it that you are successful. Entering into covenant with God is a winning situation, *because God cannot fail.*

> *Now what I am commanding you today is not too difficult for you or beyond your reach.* (Deuteronomy 30:11)

God promises that you will be blessed if you listen to Him, walk in His ways, and keep His commandments. These commandments are not so difficult that you cannot fulfill them. He is not waiting to hit you over the head with some outrageous demand of self-denial and self-abasement. God is at your side to help you reach your full potential and become a physically healthy, strong, and vigorous person. This is His part of the commitment. As you begin, carefully and prayerfully make your decision to commit yourself wholly to living God's way. This is your part of the commitment. It is a commitment to change: You will be staying on a lifetime program, not merely going on another diet. Diets don't change us. The scientific evidence is that they may only make things worse. Therefore, we will not be using the word *diet.* We will be using the word *faithful,* because we are training our eating habits through the power of the Holy Spirit and the Word of God.

The word is very near you; it is in your mouth and in your heart so you may obey it. (Deuteronomy 30:14)

Maybe you are concerned about failure—wouldn't that be "letting God down"? You *can* be faithful to Him and to His Word if you will connect your will to His. He has a great purpose for your life—that is the motivator. And His purpose always requires obedience on your part—that is the fuel. In order to reach your goal—not a weight goal, but *faithfulness*—you begin with commitment, then walk in that commitment.

See, I set before you today life and prosperity, death and destruction. For I command you today to love the Lord your God, to walk in his ways, and to keep his commands, decrees and laws; then you will live and increase, and the Lord your God will bless you in the land you are entering to possess. (Deuteronomy 30:15–16)

Expect God to help you. Expect change. You are making a commitment with the Lord today regarding how you treat your body. This commitment, or covenant, is a *binding agreement.* You are now committed to putting the Lord Jesus in a position of lordship over every area of your life, including what you eat.

Remember: You are binding yourself to the Lord, not to a plan or a program. Your new goal is to glorify and lift up Jesus in your eating.

Your commitment to freedom and getting your body into right order must be maintained daily. When our commitment is sincere, we succeed—God promises that. *So keep the words of this covenant to do them, that you may prosper in all you do.*

ADDING PRAYER TO YOUR LIFE

A life of prayer is a life of power. Communicating with the Lord is your daily power. In fact, we call our daily prayer time our Daily Power Time. At the end of each chapter in this book there will be a prayer for you to pray. Pray these out loud, and as many times as possible. Listen to yourself say the words and concentrate on what you're saying. Say the words "I choose"— and as you hear yourself speak these words, realize that you are taking a strong spiritual stand. We know that we can change the course of history, move mountains, and see miracles through the power of prayer.

You are going to see the miracle of a healthier and happier you.

PRAYER

Father, I choose to make Jesus the Lord of my life. I give my body, soul, and spirit to you now. I receive Jesus as my Savior, and I choose to live my life now by the power of the Holy Spirit.

I make a commitment to you, Lord, regarding my eating habits. I choose to put you in the position of lordship over every area of my life, particularly in the area of eating. I refuse to be a victim of overeating and poor eating.

I refuse to accept a life of defeat! I choose to commit to you, to your ways and your Word. I choose the blessing of obedience and self-control. In Jesus' name. Amen.

3

WHAT ARE YOUR MOTIVES?

The living room crackled with excitement. The women gathered there were all on *The All-New Free to Be Thin* lifestyle plan. Barbara, a tall, dark-haired woman, was speaking. "I can't tell you how wonderful it is to finally feel I can have a relationship with my sisters without it turning into another world war." The other women murmured in agreement. Many of them had already talked about their poor relationships. And many had also spoken with joy about renewed relationships with family, in-laws, and friends. "I can now face the fact that the responsibility for my choices and my behavior is mine and mine alone," Barbara confided. The smiles and nods she received told her others had made the same personal discovery.

Overeaters are often selfish people who look at self-denial as punishment rather than a necessary part of life, as well as a healthy response to the love of God. When Barbara lost 43 pounds on *The All-New Free to Be Thin* lifestyle plan, she explained, "I never realized how selfish I was. I had read about others who had changed their lives and eating habits. I had heard the talk about eating because of anger and frustration, but I guess I just went on blaming my problems on everything and everyone else. I never stopped to really look at my life. I've been full of resentment—and I've eaten my way into oblivion because of my resentments. I've hated the idea of exercise and stayed away from it."

What she shared next came with tears: "All my life I have felt inferior to my sisters because they were thin and I was overweight. I am an overweight overeater. I have been a food abuser all my life and thought I was eating to treat myself. My sisters have always tried to give me advice, which I have resented. I have been a person full of anger and jealousy! I can't thank God enough for the change in me."

The Lord is telling you, "Come to me." He is saying, "Hold on to me." He is ready to take you on the next step of your journey: making it your goal to please Him.

> *We make it our goal to please him, whether we are at home in the body or away from it.* (2 Corinthians 5:9)

What is your goal? A goal—an ambition or motive—is the *reason* behind our behaviors and actions.

When we face our selfish motives and really look at our lives, we can see the cycle of self-destruction. We design our own destinies by choosing our actions and our thoughts. The previous attempts to lose weight by all the women in Barbara's living room that night had failed. Every one had been on many diets before, and always gained back every pound. Making a firm decision to make a lifestyle change with the Lord and leaving the results to Him was the *secret to discovering a life of freedom.*

WHY AM I DOING THIS?

Let's be honest. When we go on diets it's almost always to lose weight in order to look better, right? We're under terrific pressure to *look* a certain way, and for us that includes thin and trim.

When I (Marie) was a teenager, I went to a doctor to lose 10 pounds after my ballet teacher told me I needed to be more "birdlike." The doctor put me on amphetamines and I became birdlike, all right—in fact, I nearly flew right out of this world. My mother was shocked one day when she saw my uncovered skeleton-body. I was a jumble of nerves and jitters. When she expressed loving concern, I snapped at her that I wasn't sick. I was just a healthy person with a dancer's body.

Healthy? I was dying of malnutrition and could have done irreparable damage to my heart, lungs, brain, and mind. It took months to get my body and mind back to a normal state. I wish I could say that was the only time I ever did something foolish to be thin, but that was only the beginning. A dozen diets and schemes later, I finally found peace with my body through God. Meeting and knowing Neva Coyle, writing the first *Free to Be Thin* books with her and contributing to *The All-New Free to Be*

Thin lifestyle plan, is one of the best things that's ever happened to me.

As a dancer, and then later a runner and physical fitness aficionado, I had led a life of dieting, weighing in, deprivation, and ups and downs. There were times when I would binge all day on ice cream, and then punish myself with melba toast and lettuce for a whole week. I shudder when I think of the pain I heaped on myself: the times I drank some ugly powdered drink for days to peel off five pounds for a television appearance, the water fasts to lose weight for a tinier-sized costume, starving for a week before an audition or a photo shoot. All to be *thin*—to be pleasing to the eyes of other people. The word *healthy* didn't enter the picture. What did it matter if I was half dead? I was *thin*.

A COMPLICATED MATTER

The issue of weight gain can be complex. Many people gain weight because of their dieting and binging patterns. The bottom line to weight control is moderation—being free enough to be in control. You can have a good and fulfilling lifestyle as soon as you choose.

There are some parts of the world where we'd be downright ugly if we were thin. Our skinny bodies would represent our poverty of spirit and reflect an inability to please God. After all, one of God's blessings to us is food. We need food to survive. It stands to reason, then, that in some cultures the heavier a person is, the more beautiful. Fat is a sign of prosperity and blessing. But you probably don't know too many people who think that way—including your doctor.

What about you? What are your thoughts about your own body?

Now is the time to examine your motives seriously. At one point I (Marie) had to make the decision to stop pursuing *thinness* and become dedicated to health and wholeness instead. I started by dealing with my eating habits. I had to carefully examine them, record what, when, and why I ate, and face myself and my habits honestly. My life changed. So can yours. Traditionally, the weight-loss industry has dealt with weight control in terms of its symptoms and excess fat. It has exploited our cultural fear of being fat, and hardly addressed an individual's reason for food abuse.

This may seem like radical advice, but in order to face compulsions that drive your overeating, you need to reject dieting for the purpose of weight-loss only, once and for all. Most of us do not gain weight because we can't stick to a diet. We gain weight, generally speaking, because we overeat and abuse our bodies. And most of the time we are unaware of what we're doing to ourselves.

If your motive has been to lose weight *so* that you can look good *so* that you can feel good about yourself, you need to take note of this: Research shows that extreme food restrictions may lead to overreaction and a fear of food. A food abuser may be threatened with the presence of food, and therefore choose to "drink" meals or eat nothing but lettuce and carrots or diet bars. If the drive is strong, normal eating eventually becomes impossible. Some people, out of their powerlessness over food, will even resort to surgery such as the *jejunoileal* bypass, stomach stapling, and vertical banded gastroplasty.

As we seek a new way of life, it's important to know what motivates us. What makes us want to change? What is that certain inner push that moves us toward a higher level of life?

MOTIVE INVENTORY

Here are some questions to ask yourself about your motives. Take enough time to answer honestly:

1. When did I go on my first diet? What were the circumstances?
2. How many weight-loss schemes have I tried in my life?
3. What is the longest period of time I've kept weight off after losing on diets?
4. When have I been the healthiest in my life? The unhealthiest?
5. When has my body been the strongest? The weakest?
6. What does physical fitness mean to me?
7. Is my body as strong now as it can be? Why or why not?

Some of us may have a struggle admitting that we were the strongest when as children we used to walk to school and play outside. One man confessed tearfully that the healthiest he had probably ever felt was as a toddler, before he began a lifelong pattern of food abuse and obesity.

If your body is not at its peak strength, why not? No excuses now. Don't give us that story about your weak back or your bad knees. Consider a woman named Sharon, for example. Sharon, now in her early forties, was stricken with polio as a child. As a result, she has never walked. Her life has been spent in a wheelchair and yet she is a strong, physically fit person. Sharon does not abuse food or allow food to abuse her. She works out daily with a program specifically designed for her capabilities. She knows her body and what it is capable of, and she is proud of who she is.

HOW DO YOU RELATE TO YOUR BODY?

How many times have you said this: "I look *terrible*," or "I could never do that, I'm too *clumsy*," or "I'm such a *klutz*," or "I *hate* my body"?

To live at peace with your body you must respect it. On *The All-New Free to Be Thin* lifestyle plan, you are going to become reacquainted with that body of yours—you're going to become friends with it and learn how to live happily and in peace with it.

"I never dreamed I could love who I am," wrote Pamela from London, England. "Self-hate was my way of life. I was on the verge of suicide before I found your book. God has done a completely new work in my heart and body. An altogether new woman lives in my body. I'm just not the same. I'm no longer a food abuser because I learned a lifestyle that I can handle. How can I ever thank you?"

Coming to peace with your body requires listening, responding, and caring enough to learn its capabilities and limitations.

YOUR MAIN MOTIVE

Make your main motive to feast on God's precious Word:

Who shall separate us from the love of Christ? Shall trouble or hardship or persecution or famine or nakedness or danger or sword? (Romans 8:35)

What shall separate us from the love of God? Shall overeating, lethargy, self-pity, alienation from others, physical limitations, hurt feelings?

What can separate us from Christ's love? Can food abuse, pigging out on unhealthy junk food? Can lying in bed all day with an overeater's hangover? Can a bag of chocolate chip cookies? Can sugary non-fat yogurt and granola bars? (Both high in calories.)

In all these things we are more than conquerors through him who loved us. (Romans 8:37)

PRAYER

Heavenly Father, help me to learn about my body and its needs. Show me what is good and what is not good for me. Show me how to value myself and how to treat myself with the loving care you want me to. I choose to stop abusing my body now in the name of Jesus. Amen.

4

HAPPILY MOTIVATED

Do everything without complaining or arguing, that you may become blameless and pure, children of God without fault in a crooked and depraved generation, in which you shine like stars in the universe. (Philippians 2:14–15)

That's us—blameless and innocent and above reproach in the midst of an overeating and junk-food laden generation!

Making a lifestyle change as you are right now takes some getting used to. Be good to yourself, allowing from one to three weeks to adjust to new choices. In the past you may have groaned and complained when you said no to an ugly greasy morsel, but now your motives are in order. You will find yourself *happy* to finally be free from bondage to overeating and poor eating. What once looked good to you will no longer hold the same appeal.

You will discover with your new motives to please the Lord that there is a new power within you. You will feel good about yourself and your choices. You will lose your old, unhealthy cravings and become excited about being healthy.

DO I HAVE TO BE THIN TO BE LOVED BY YOU?

If you're like the rest of the human race, your motives for losing weight in the past were probably to look better. Then you weren't concerned as much about your attributes of intelligence, wisdom, kindness, goodness, talent, strength, courage—you just wanted to go for *thin*! One woman in deep need of spiritual enlightenment told us, "Thin is really what counts when you want to attract the opposite sex, right?" Then she added, "A thin body and big breasts are all I need to get a man." A sad commentary on the way women have come to think of their bodies, and the way advertising has exploited us!

Then again, how many brides have you spoken to who did *not* try to lose weight before the wedding? "I wish men suffered like us women," a young newlywed woman complained. "How many grooms do you know who starve themselves before the wedding to fit into their tux?" This says something about the source of our self-image, doesn't it? Women traditionally have looked for their self-worth in outward appearance.

If you're a woman, ask yourself: Is it my appearance that permits me to be loved by a man? Is it my appearance that defines me as feminine? Does my weight tell me if I'm desirable or not? Since ancient times, women have been valued by their outward beauty. Even Queen Esther in the Bible was made queen not because she was clever with numbers or had a real talent for running countries, but because she was a beauty contest winner. Only incidentally, and fortunately for us, was she a godly and highly intelligent young woman. But if Queen Esther had had uncontrollable eating problems, the history of the Jewish nation would be entirely different today.

Face it—humans can be awfully shallow.

Mary lost 15 pounds for her high school reunion. She wanted to look as good as she did in high school—and she wanted to "show up" several of the other more popular girls who were now fat and dowdy. The day after the reunion she ate . . . and ate . . . and ate. Two months later she had gained back not only the 15 pounds she'd lost, but 7 more on top of that.

Monica lost 35 pounds before her wedding—but lost control and ate three pieces of wedding cake at the reception. And she did not stop eating until, three months later, she had gained 40 pounds.

Do you see how important your motives are?

Do nothing out of selfish ambition or vain conceit. (Philippians 2:3)

There is nothing wrong with wanting to look attractive. In fact, when a person becomes a Christian, he or she usually gains a new attractiveness and vibrancy. The life within gives a radiance that wasn't there before.

The Holy Spirit gives new motivation to the Christian to be attractive and feel attractive. When selfish and vain motives creep in, the natural working of the Lord is hindered. Did you know that you can stifle God's work in your life when you habitually engage in a behavior that makes you feel ashamed? Those days can be over—now!

Delight yourself in Me. I shall fulfill the desires of your heart. (Psalm 37:4, paraphrased)

The Lord will fulfill your desires. This is His promise to you. Whether you are a woman or a man, God wants to make you beautiful. He will do it—if you let Him.

NEW POWER-THOUGHTS

- I use food. Food does not use me.
- I am in control over what goes into my body.
- I am *free* from binging, gluttony, and overeating.
- I am healthier, more energetic, and in *control* of my life.
- I am no longer selfishly indulging in food.
- I am turning to God for my needs and desires to be fulfilled.

As your motives to please the Lord become stronger and stronger, you will see Him work from the inside out. Once your motives are in the proper place within your heart, you will begin to see permanent change.

It is God who works in you . . . according to his good purpose. (Philippians 2:13)

Jesus is our role model. He shows us how to choose right motivation.

And being found in appearance as a man, he humbled himself and became obedient to death—even death on a cross! Therefore God exalted him to the highest place and gave him the name that is above every name. (Philippians 2:8–9)

Jesus did not come to earth to do whatever He felt like doing. He didn't choose a life of chance or self-indulgence. He lived in constant obedience to His Father.

It is God who works in you . . . according to his good purpose.

He wants to perform His perfect will in *you* and in your *life*— to fulfill His purpose for your life. Your motive is to *please Him.*

God is not punishing you when He helps you to say no to ugly foods. He is *blessing* you with a new lifestyle and lovingly showing you how to walk in the power of His Spirit.

Prayer

Father, I choose now a changed lifestyle for your sake. I give up the old motives that have in the past failed. I choose now to glorify you. Show me new insight and direction into your will for my body. In Jesus' name. Amen.

5

ON YOUR WAY TO A HEALTHIER YOU

You have given your appetite and your eating habits to the Lord. You are on your way to an entirely new way of eating and living. You're on your way to a new you!

Don't you know that you yourselves are God's temple and that God's Spirit lives in you? (1 Corinthians 3:16)

The Lord Jesus and the Word of God are directing your motives for a healthier life. You will now be making your body—*your temple*—stronger and healthier. What a wonderful temple for the Holy Spirit to dwell in—a strong, firm, and healthy body, not one that is overstuffed and unable to move at His direction.

In order to be healthier and to serve God, then, your new goal must be to feed strength and vigor into your body. Instead of the overfed and undernourished body you've been accustomed to, you want to feel lighter, fresher, and more energetic. Then you will begin to get a sense of the value of God's holy temple. You will begin to feel like a vessel fit for the Master's use. You will be making wise decisions, ones that will help you to feel more energetic, happier, and healthier.

When Jesus was preaching along the Sea of Galilee, a great crowd of people were following Him. They were excited and awed at the signs and wonders the Lord was performing. Sick people were being healed, the lame were walking. It was one of the most thrilling spectacles they'd ever seen!

Then Jesus went up on a mountain and sat down with His disciples for a bit. Since they were out away from the town, Jesus was concerned that the people needed to eat. He looked up and saw the masses coming toward them. He knew they had been following Him in the heat and dust, pressing together in the great crowds, and they were hungry. As always, His concern was for the *people.*

> He said to Philip, *"Where shall we buy bread for these peo-ple to eat?"* (John 6:5)

Notice he didn't suggest honey cakes. He didn't say, "Where are we going to buy candy bars so these people can get some quick energy?"

If you think the Lord is eager to have you eat fattening sweets for energy, you may want to do some more reading of the Word: God does not starve His beloved children with sugary foods that do not nourish the body. He doesn't prescribe greasy, salty foods—which actually rob you of energy. As one woman aptly put it, "If Jesus were here today, would you see Him coming out of a supermarket with 12 bags of potato chips, one for each dis-ciple?"

> Then you will know the truth, and the truth will set you free. (John 8:32)

The disciples didn't have enough money to buy bread for the great host of people who were gathered that day. It was Andrew who told the Lord, "Here is a boy with five small barley loaves and two small fish" (John 6:9).

This pleased Jesus. "Have the people sit down," He said. They were going to have a feast. And the feast for this hungry and tired crowd was an all-you-can-eat, high-fiber, high-protein meal. Jesus took the loaves and thanked God for them. He dis-tributed to those who were sitting down, then did the same with the fish. Everybody ate as much as they wanted, and there were 12 baskets left over, filled with pieces of the 5 barley loaves. The Lord multiplied a nutritious meal for the people.

Wouldn't it be great to have the Lord take charge of your meals?

The Lord is by your side right now to help you as you make new choices. He will multiply your desire for good foods. He will perform a miracle in your life. Your goal, remember, is to eat in obedience to God through the power of the Holy Spirit. The Lord's help comes through your willingness to be completely His. Your attitudes have to match His will for you. Your com-mitment to Him has to be complete, your goals His goals, your attention given to hearing from Him and obeying Him.

You cannot fail when you give yourself completely to God and allow Him to gently teach you His ways.

Those who live according to the sinful nature have their minds set on what that nature desires; but those who live in accordance with the Spirit have their minds set on what the Spirit desires. (Romans 8:5)

EXPECT RESULTS

When you pray and give your eating habits to the Lord, you can expect wonderful results. First you give your life, your entire being to Him. You become totally His, surrendered to Him and to walking in His ways. Then you observe your desires, appetites, longings, dreams, ideas, and thoughts are more united with the Lord. Your mind becomes set on the things of the Spirit. You are a spiritual person and you see a difference in your life!

The mind of sinful man is death, but the mind controlled by the Spirit is life and peace. . . . You, however, are controlled not by the sinful nature but by the Spirit, if the Spirit of God lives in you. (Romans 8:6, 9)

What tangible results can you expect regarding your eating?

You will no longer turn to food when you are frustrated, nervous, or worried. If you feel rejected and unloved, food will not be your comfort. If you feel bored and depressed, food will not relieve you. These emotions are triggers for food abuse. Turn to the Word of God and fill your mind with its power, wisdom, and strength. The Word of God is powerful and alive. When you read the Scriptures and concentrate on the words, the Holy Spirit unites himself through the words to your spirit and the words become alive in you. They breathe life and truth into your entire being.

You will discover amazing inner strength and peace through the Word. Concentrate on it; meditate on it. This will help you to remain in wonderful communion with the Lord.

The sinful mind is hostile to God. It does not submit to God's law, nor can it do so. Those controlled by the sinful nature cannot please God. (Romans 8:7–8)

The many times you have tried to change your habits in your own strength, without God, are in the past now. Ask God's forgiveness for those futile attempts. You receive God's blessings by knowing and doing His will for you. Now you are no longer deceived. You know God wants to help. You know He loves and cares for your body and is right beside you helping and blessing you.

> *And if the Spirit of him who raised Jesus from the dead is living in you, he who raised Christ from the dead will also give life to your mortal bodies through his Spirit, who lives in you.* (Romans 8:11)

If the Spirit of God could raise Jesus Christ from the dead, He can surely help you! You have a powerhouse of strength within you to help you overcome overeating. When you begin to tap the resources within you, you will soar with new energy and willpower.

You Are in Control

> *Therefore do not let anyone judge you by what you eat or drink. . . . These are a shadow of the things that were to come; the reality, however, is found in Christ.* (Colossians 2:16, 17)

This means that you are in control of your eating habits through the power of the Holy Spirit. If you look at your past eating habits, you will probably see that when you were out of control, it was because you didn't plan what you ate. You didn't care what you ate. Now the Lord is giving you self-control. Your best friend may say to you tonight, "Oh, go ahead and have that piece of pie. I baked it just for you! One little piece of pie can't hurt." Then your natural, people-pleasing thoughts may tell you that you are in a situation where you have no power to choose— but that is not the truth. You can diplomatically explain why this would be a poor choice for you and ask for understanding.

If your friend really cares about you, she or he will respect your new food choices. Your desire is to please the Lord with your eating habits. It's up to you. Remain firm in your choices. In time your friends will understand when you refuse foods and negative habits that are not part of your new lifestyle.

Ann comes from a large Italian family that loves to eat. When Ann came to her first *Free to Be Thin* group meeting she had 80 extra pounds on her small frame. She told how the meaty, oily pasta sauces and rich desserts had always been part of her life. Now she was living on her own and cooking healthy, low-fat, low-calorie meals herself. Going home was always a trial because her mother insisted she "have another helping," or "eat your dessert—I made it just for you, and it's your favorite!"

In Ann's *Free to Be Thin* lifestyle plan, she had to learn how to be assertive with herself as well as the people in her life. She learned to tell her mother point-blank, "Mama, I am a food abuser. We are both Christians, and so I know you will understand. I want to please the Lord, and that means changing my eating habits. That's why I am saying *no* to another helping of lasagna—and I won't have dessert. But I'm so thankful that you love me and want me to enjoy the foods I used to eat without restriction."

Ann's mother pouted—but for only a moment. She gained respect for Ann and eventually asked questions about her new life-change. Ann's mother herself is a typical food abuser. Feeding someone rich and fattening foods was her way of expressing love. Ann had to show her mother that food was not what she wanted as an expression of love. Both Ann and her mother began to learn to express their love in other ways.

PLEASE DON'T ASK ME TO FAIL

Friends may tell you: "Come on and splurge a little. It won't hurt to go off your program just this once!" It may be a temptation to listen to them and do as they suggest. You may tell yourself that tomorrow you'll start again. There's always *tomorrow.*

Friends may say, "Oh, come on—you can do your walk later," or, "Can't your exercise wait for another time? Do it *tomorrow.*"

You don't have to sink into temptation! Tomorrow is a long way off. Today is your treasure. You can rise above the temptation to fall into old habits.

You are living a *new* life of discipline and self-control. The food may be very tempting, but you *don't* have to eat it. You are choosing healthy, good foods for your body now. You're choosing a healthier, more active lifestyle.

"No," you will answer. "I will not splurge. I will not eat that. Please don't ask me to fail."

DIETS THAT HURT

Do not let anyone who delights in false humility . . . disqualify you for the prize. (Colossians 2:18)

When you are changing your eating habits with the Lord's help and encouragement, you will not degrade yourself or your body. The reason is that you are now more aware of His love for you. He cares deeply for you and for the health and vitality of your physical body. You are now eating to please Him. You won't defile or hurt something that is a gift from God.

Your body is precious to the Lord. Here are some ways your body can be hurt. Avoid them!

1. *Fad diets.* Diets that require you to eat only one kind of food, such as a grapefruit diet or a banana diet or an all-protein diet, are harmful and dangerous to your body.

A young woman sat sullenly in a *Free to Be Thin* group meeting, her eyes glazed, staring straight ahead at the leader. She was definitely not overweight—in fact, she was underweight and looked gaunt and undernourished. She also had a distant and faraway look in her eye, as though she were in a daze.

After the meeting she asked to speak privately to the group leader. She told her she had recently lost 65 pounds on predigested liquid protein. Now she was suffering heart tissue damage and nervous disorders. Furthermore, she was afraid to eat. She had been fat all her life and she worried that she'd gain it all back if she started eating again.

This woman, like many others we have talked to, is one of countless now-thin people soon to be fat again because of fad or extreme dieting methods.

God does not hurt our bodies, damage our hearts, and destroy our personalities. He wants to bless our lives. He does not fill us with fear or anxiety about eating. He beautifully and sweetly teaches us how to eat properly so that we will never again be in bondage to food.

2. *Fasting.* Going without food—especially with mixed motives—can be just as drastic for the overeater as binging. It is an extreme behavior, just as overeating is an extreme behavior.

Many hospitals and physicians use a fasting method for weight loss and gradually wean the person back on to a calorie-restricted eating program. There will be a large weight loss in the beginning of the program; later, additional weight will be lost gradually.

You will lose weight on a fast, but this kind of weight-loss is not permanent. During the early stages of a fast, you will lose as much lean body tissue as you do fat. This loss may result in the arrest of hair growth and/or the development of scaly skin.

Be warned: Metabolic disturbances on a fast can endanger health and life. These disturbances include the depletion of various body salts, the buildup of uric acid (which can damage the kidneys and cause the painful arthritis known as gout), and cause dangerous heart rhythm problems. Total fasting results in breakdown of muscle tissue—including the heart.[1]

The protein-sparing modified fast, usually supervised by a physician, is a very low-calorie diet, supplying only 400 to 800 calories per day. The diet is usually in a powdered form mixed in a blender with water and ice and calorie-free flavorings. The dieter is supposed to lose between two to four pounds per week. Although some of the programs include a weekly follow-up group plan aimed at behavior modification, nutritional counseling, and physical activity, the people who have lost weight on this plan almost always regain it and add more on. One five-year study has shown only three percent of the patients managed to keep off a portion of the weight they had lost. These radical methods of weight loss miss the point: They do not get at the root cause of the overeater's problem. They treat the symptom and not the cause.

> *Since you died with Christ to the basic principles of this world, why, as though you still belonged to it, do you submit to its rules: "Do not handle! Do not taste! Do not touch!"?*
> *. . . Such regulations indeed have an appearance of wisdom, with their self-imposed worship, their false humility and their harsh treatment of the body, but they lack any value in restraining sensual indulgence.* (Colossians 2:20–21, 23)

Many people fast for the purpose of prayer and intercession. This is a spiritual practice and one that should be engaged in without a thought of weight loss.

---

[1]Lynn J. Bennien, M.D., Edwin L. Bierman, M.D., and James M. Ferguson, M.D., "Straight Talk About Weight Control," *Consumer Book Report* (New York: Consumers Union, 1991).

3. *Sugary drugs, pills, powders, candies, diet bars, and gums are not options.* The lasting way to lose weight and keep it off is to change your eating habits. In desperation to lose weight, some choose painful and dangerous bypass surgery. In addition to the painful and tedious recovery, the surgery is effective for only five years. For some it doesn't last that long.

You can't cut out your thinking with a knife. You can't remove overeating habits with a pill or a candy before a meal, or a powdered drink instead of a meal. You can't end the painful grip of food abuse over your life with a shot or drugs. Eventually, overeating will rear its head again and you will be once again eating poorly.

The more often you go through times of weight loss, the more difficult it is to maintain that weight loss. With every diet you go on, your body struggles to replace the lost weight. Fat cells will actually work to maintain their own expanded size. The more weight you lose with the radical dieting and weight-loss methods, the faster your weight is liable to return and the more difficult it will be to shed in your next attempt. It is heartbreaking and frustrating, to say the least.

He who began a good work in you will carry it on to completion until the day of Christ Jesus. (Philippians 1:6)

He is not going to allow you to fail.

First, as we have said, you must forsake the fad diet and restrictive programs you have attempted in the past, realizing they have not worked. These questionable programs, diets, and devices—with their false promises—are of no value against overeating.

In the next chapters you are going to learn about your body type and how to eat specifically for your own body and lifestyle. You will also learn to choose what kinds of foods are best for you.

PRAYER

Dear Lord, I repent of my past destructive eating patterns and return to your ways. I come into your arms now. Forgive me, Lord, for not taking the strength and wisdom you so freely and readily give. I know you love me dearly, Lord, and for that reason I will not hurt or destroy my body. I will bless my body in the name of Jesus.

I am a conqueror, in the name of Jesus Christ. I now begin a new way of eating and living according to the Word of God and the power of the Holy Spirit. I turn from the old, useless ways to the new, bright, and beautiful. My hope is in the Lord, not in diets and devices.

I hereby refuse to put my trust in fad diets, fasting, pills, drugs, surgery, or any other false promise. I declare myself free.

I am now free!

In Jesus' name. Amen.

6

MY BODY, MY SELF

YOUR BASIC BODY TYPE

How well do you really know yourself?

The psychology of *relating body type to temperament* is known as constitutional psychology. Its chief proponent has been William Sheldon, a gifted physician as well as psychologist. Sheldon's *somatotypes* and their personality traits are well known, and they are placed in three general classifications: the endomorph, the mesomorph, and the ectomorph.

Sheldon proposes that when one of these dimensions predominates, a person can be identified as an *endomorph* (fleshy and soft body type), a *mesomorph* (strong and athletic type), or an *ectomorph* (long and slender body type). By a rating procedure known as *somatotyping,* a person is scored on a seven-point scale to see which of these traits is most dominant in his or her physique.

Almost no one fits a perfect description of one category alone. We are all a percentage of each. You may be 25 percent endomorph, 75 percent mesomorph. Or you may be 90 percent mesomorph, 10 percent ectomorph. Whatever your dominant body type is, you'll have a combination of two.

Are you large or small boned? You may weigh more than an ideal weight chart says you should, and *still* look tiny. Your bone structure tells you how much you should weigh. If you have large bones, you should weigh in at the heavy end of the recommended range for your height.

To find out whether your bones are large or small, measure your wrist an inch above the bony part. Divide your height by this measurement. If it goes more than twelve times, you probably have light bones. Less than eleven times, your bones are on the heavy side.

Endomorphy   *Mesomorphy*   *Ectomorphy*

Understanding your basic body type is very important. You may be putting harsh demands upon yourself to be something that you never will be. Or, if you do reach your impossible standard, it will be a grueling and futile task to maintain that size. A case in point is Kelly, a professional ice skater who joined a *Free to Be Thin* group ten years ago and has maintained her weight loss of twenty-two pounds.

"The maintaining part was always the hardest of any weight-loss plan I've ever tried," Kelly told her group. "But the *Free to Be Thin* program showed me how to get my priorities straight. I've learned how to *eat,* not diet."

When Kelly first came to the group, she wrote on her goal sheet that she wanted to get down to 100 pounds. She weighed 146 pounds at the time. She tells us, "In my teen years as a skater I fought and struggled with my weight every day of my life. Other skaters I knew could eat ice cream and heaps of french fries and other foods I stayed away from, and yet they remained skinny! But my bones are heavy, like the mesomorph, and I don't burn calories easily. Also, being slim is not my nature, as it is for the ectomorph. For me, the *All-New Free to Be Thin* lifestyle is perfect because it has taught me how to know and appreciate my own unique self and how to eat specifically for my body type."

Kelly, who is lean and muscular, weighs between 124 and 125 now. She feels much happier with herself than when she was a teenager. "God has guided me every step of the way in realizing how precious I am to Him," she told us. "He formed me, and my body type is special to Him. I realize it is my responsibility to know and appreciate my body. I've stopped hating and punishing myself. I treat myself with care now that I am food-educated. A big bonus is, I'm skating better than ever."

Take time now to determine your body type. Fit this into your new way of thinking:

- I have a predominately _____ body type.
- It is beautiful in the sight of God because He created and formed me.
- I accept my body, my bones, muscles, tissues—all of it.
- I *appreciate* my body.
- I will not make impossible demands on my body. I will treat it with respect and care.

THE THIN FOOD ABUSER

Kelly's friends could eat sugar-drenched junk foods and eat saturated animal fats without gaining weight—but remember, weight is not the criteria for good health. The friends she speaks of, ectomorph body types, seem to be able to eat whatever they want and stay slim. But they may be starving themselves nutritionally. Worse, a diet of processed foods and sugar drinks can produce nutrition-deficiency symptoms such as anxiety, irritability, diarrhea, headaches, bad breath, fatigue, loss of body protein, anemia, hypoglycemia, and more.[1]

On the other end of the health spectrum, Kelly, who is a predominantly mesomorph body type, is in constant control of her eating. She is aware and informed. She has worked hard at understanding herself and her body's needs. Now she concentrates on health, *not* thinness.

The overweight food abuser and the thin food abuser share a common malady: They're both unhealthy. The thin food abuser may have habits similar to the overweight food abuser in that he or she may go on food binges and then follow with not eating at all.

People with the eating disorders *anorexia* and *bulimia* are often those with thin body types. Anorexics starve themselves without food while bulimics starve by vomiting the food eaten. Some anorexics are deathly looking skeletons. Bulimics take on

---

[1]Michigan Health Council, 1990.

a sickly color, broken blood vessels appear on their faces and they are nervous and volatile.

YOUR WONDERFUL BODY

Each of us is an individual, highly unique and important to the Lord. He gives each of us our bodies and created them perfectly and specifically according to His perfect design and measurement. It is important for you to hear Him give you His own custom-made instructions and directions for your own body.

After you have learned your body type, you will want to determine what your daily food intake should be to (a) lose weight and become healthier, and (b) maintain your new improved health and weight.

Once again, you are not learning to diet; you are learning to *eat.* You will be learning how to be a friend of food instead of an abuser of food. *The All-New Free to Be Thin* lifestyle plan is not a fad program.

Your body needs approximately 40 different nutrients to stay healthy. These include vitamins and minerals, as well as amino acids (from proteins), essential fatty acids (from vegetable oils), and sources of energy (calories from carbohydrates, protein, and fat).

No single food will supply all the essential nutrients in the amount your body requires. You will be eating a wonderful and endless variety and combination of foods.

NO MORE COUNTING CALORIES

That's right! No more counting calories. Although you won't need to keep a calorie chart, you will need a basic knowledge of what the calorie is and its value for your age, body type, and lifestyle.

Energy available in food is measured by calories. Food provides the energy we need to breathe, digest food, and maintain body heat in order to sustain the body functions that comprise our basal metabolism, or basic life processes. Age lowers our basal metabolism, and that's why older people require fewer calories. You need calories to keep your body functioning and to supply you with energy for the muscular activity you do each day.

Calories are equal, no matter where they come from. Energy, whether coming from a piece of cake or a sirloin steak, is equal in that energy not used by the body is stored in the form of fat.

Food abusers often do not take time to learn about nutrition. They may not want to know that the foods they crave are bad for the body. One woman went to a luncheon and ate the most fattening foods on the menu, telling herself and others, "Oh, this is okay. After all, everything I'm eating is natural." The greasy lasagna was "natural" with fatty meat, egg noodles, cheese, salt, and empty calories. The carrot cake she ate for dessert had "natural" eggs, cream, butter—all things that she insisted were "healthy and natural."

She couldn't be more *wrong*. The nutrients were cooked or processed out of the food, so the benefits to her were nil. And the calories soared: The one meal she ate held a walloping 2,000 calories, mostly from worthless fat.

Calories measure energy. Since fat has more than twice as many calories as carbohydrates and proteins, take care to eat foods that are low in fat and high in complex carbohydrates (vegetables and whole grain) and protein.

The following formula is a method for determining your calorie needs per day.[2] Remember, these calories are to be found in *whole foods eaten for their nutrients.* In one day, you could consume nothing but four pieces of cake and two colas and possibly stay within your calorie limit—but you would have starved your bones, lungs, blood cells, brain, skin, tissue, and muscles.

What are your daily calorie needs? (See chart on page 44.)

The Mirror Test

Now, the moment of truth, for some of us: *Find a full-length mirror and look into it.* If you are like some overweight food abusers, you may not even own a full-length mirror. In that case, before we go further, sit down in a chair and get quiet.

Can you say:

I am fearfully and wonderfully made.

I accept myself.

I accept and bless my body.

I will eat and care for my health because I am precious.

---

[2]As quoted in *Overcoming the Dieting Dilemma* by Neva Coyle (Minneapolis: Bethany House Publishers, 1991).

Normal Daily Calorie Needs

Women:

1. Begin with a base of 655 calories   655
2. Multiply your weight (in pounds) × 4.3   _____
3. Multiply your height (in inches) × 4.7   _____
4. Add together the totals from
       #1, #2, and #3   _____
5. Multiply your age × 4.7   _____
6. Subtract #5 from #4   _____
       (Your normal resting metabolic rate)
7. Multiply result of #6 × 1.1   _____
8. Round off #7 to the nearest 100
       (your daily calories)   _____

Men:

1. Begin with a base of 66 calories   66
2. Multiply your weight (in pounds) × 6.3   _____
3. Multiply your height (in inches) × 12.7   _____
4. Add together the totals from
       #1, #2 and #3   _____
5. Multiply your age by 6.8   _____
6. Subtract #5 from #4   _____
       (Your normal resting metabolic rate)
7. Multiply result of #6 × 1.1   _____
8. Round off #7 to nearest 100
       (your daily calories)*   _____

As quoted in *Overcoming the Dieting Dilemma* by Neva Coyle (Minneapolis: Bethany House Publishers, 1991).

I choose not to abuse myself in any way.

My body was created to be healthy, and I will cooperate with God to make it so.

God is speaking words of love to you right now. Can you hear them?

I have loved you with an everlasting love; I have drawn you with loving-kindness. (Jeremiah 31:3)

PRAYER

Heavenly Father, I thank you for my body. I thank you for creating me exactly the way you did. Show me how to take care of this precious body you have given me. I choose to bless my body because you love me with an everlasting love. You have fearfully and wonderfully made me, and I thank you. Amen.

7

Gain Back Your Energy With a New Way to Eat

Many overeaters say they do not ever remember being truly energetic. "I've always been a slow mover," one overeater reports. "It runs in my family," says another. But what ran in both of these families was overeating.

At the root of a lack of energy, for many of us, is a lifetime of food abuse.

When asked to name "energy foods," many people list chocolate and other sugary foods. Most, if they want a quick energy pickup, reach for coffee or a diet cola.

Let's understand something right now: Sugar and caffeine are not energy foods! They give you absolutely nothing but a momentary jolt—and they rob you of plenty.

Earlier we established our calorie needs and made a promise not to be ruled by counting calories. What we *do* need to become aware of is the *fat content* in our foods. We also need to become aware of good and bad *carbohydrates,* and how much *protein* we need versus what we eat. So, we will use calories to compute food exchanges, and also as a barometer for understanding what we put into our bodies. But to build a new lifestyle of healthy eating, we will rely on our *food choices.*

Are Carbohydrates Our Friends?

A gram of fat contains approximately nine calories. A gram of carbohydrates contains approximately four calories. Do you remember when you thought all carbohydrates were bad, so you ate cottage cheese instead of a baked potato? Those days are gone! Potatoes are *good* carbohydrates and you should include them in your food plan.

Good carbohydrates are *complex* carbohydrates. They are:

Vegetables—both raw and cooked, including those you always thought were too fattening to eat, such as potatoes, sweet potatoes, corn, squash, yams, and peas. (But while losing weight, limit these and keep portions small.)

Legumes—including lentils, black beans, kidney beans, Great Northern beans, garbanzo beans, red beans, soybeans, split peas;

Breads—only whole grain, low-fat, unsalted; avoid white flour products of any kind, matzohs, pita, corn tortillas, water and flour bagels, and crackers such as Rye-Krisp.

Cereals—whole grain *only* (without sugar or other additives), including wheat bran, oat bran, oatmeal, wheat meal;

Pastas—wheat and vegetable only, not the egg and white flour type;

Grains—brown rice, bulgur, millet, barley, rye, corn.

Bad carbohydrates are *refined* carbohydrates. They can be found in:

White flour products, including breads, rolls, muffins, cakes, breadsticks, salted, oily crackers, pies, pizza dough, egg noodles, doughnuts, biscuits, dumplings, egg bagels, croissants, pancakes, waffles, English muffins, buns, chips;

Cake and cookie mixes

Store bought cookies, packaged snacks and pastries, rolls;

Prepared one-dish meals, TV dinners and frozen meals;

Breakfast cereal (refined, sugary, without whole grain)

Fast foods—hamburgers, cheeseburgers, fish sticks, fried and breaded meats, tacos, burritos, pizza, processed luncheon meats, including chicken and turkey.

Complex carbohydrates will *not* add fat to your body!

It is recommended that 60 percent of our total calorie intake come from *complex carbohydrates.* The remaining 40 percent should come from protein and fat.

WHAT FATS ARE YOU EATING?

You need to become aware of *fat content* in the foods you eat. You will now be alerted to the foods that are low fat, and substitute them for the high-fat foods you may have been eating.

Studies show that the average woman losing weight should consume only 20 to 30 grams of fat per day. The average man losing weight should have 30 to 60 grams of fat per day.

Because we want you to succeed, we want you to examine where you are getting your calories from. And so, it is important to look at the various sources of fat in your diet.

Animal fat is mono-saturated fat. It's the kind of fat that encourages the body to increase its production of cholesterol. Saturated fat is *solid* fat. It clogs and clings—it's the worst. Mono-saturated fat is found in all red meat, including hamburger, sausage, steak, ham, pork, veal, and lamb. It is also found in butter, whole milk, cheese, and egg yolks, which are all high in saturated fatty acids.

Fat from palm, palm kernel oil, cocoa butter, and coconut oil is highly saturated fat. These oils should be avoided! These saturated fats are found in candy bars, egg substitutes, non-dairy creamers and processed foods, to name a few. Read labels carefully.

Vegetable oil contains fat that is polyunsaturated, and comes from fruits and seeds. It is *liquid* at room temperature. Nutritional and medical experts tell us some vegetable oils—such as olive oil—actually help lower cholesterol levels. These oils are good oils—taken in moderation, of course. The most common polyunsaturates are found in corn and safflower oils.

The American Heart Association has recommended limiting the consumption of polyunsaturated oils in its recommendation to reduce the intake of all fats—so don't be fooled by the advertisements for margarines, vegetable oils, and food products marked "cholesterol free." This simply means the fat in the product is not animal fat. Some products urge you to eat *more* polyunsaturated fats for your health! Highly processed margarine, for example, contains partially hydrogenated vegetable oils that actually contain *more* saturated fat than the original oil because of the hydrogenation process.

Remember, *all* fats are a highly concentrated source of calories. Olive oil is still 100 percent fat. One tablespoon contains 14 grams of fat, the same as one tablespoon of bacon fat. (Don't misunderstand, though: The bacon fat also contains 3.6 grams of solid saturated fat, 9 milligrams of cholesterol, and 126 milligrams of sodium!)

So where should the fat we eat come from? Nutrition experts tell us now that most of our daily intake of fat should be from vegetables, fruits, and grain. A small amount of fat should be from fish, fowl, and lean meats, and only 8 percent from dairy products. Remember, *foods highest in fat are meat and dairy products.*

KNOW YOUR FAT AND CHOLESTEROL

Limit your daily intake of cholesterol to less than 300 milligrams

COMPARE:

Bad News			Good News		
Food	*Grams of Fat*	*mg. of cholesterol*	*Food*	*Grams of Fat*	*mg. of cholesterol*
French Fries	16.0	14	Baked Potato	2.0	0
Carrot cake (3½ oz.)	20.4	30	Whole-wheat bread, 1 slice	.8	0
Ice cream (1 C. 16% fat)	23.8	84	Frozen yogurt (1 C.)	3.0	10
Ricotta cheese (½ C. 13% fat)	16.1	63	Cottage cheese (non-fat)	1.6	5
Yogurt (1 C. whole milk)	7.7	30	Yogurt (1 C. no-fat)	3.4	14
Whole egg	5.5	250	Egg White	0*	0
Butter (1 Tbsp.)	12.2	36			
Ground beef (3 oz. 27% fat)	16.9	86	Sole	9.8	42
Chicken liver (1 C.)	4.4	746	Chicken (3 oz. white)	4.2	66
Mayonnaise (1 Tbsp.)	11.0	5	No-oil salad dressing	0	0

*Trace source USDA

ENERGY, NOT LETHARGY

What does this information on cholesterol, fats, and carbohydrates have to do with having more energy? Carbohydrates give you long-lasting fuel for energy. They provide the brain with its primary fuel. After the body breaks down the carbohydrates into usable units of sugar molecules or glucose, only carbon dioxide and water remain, which we expel through our lungs by breathing.

Carbohydrates are low in fat and provide generous amounts of vitamins, minerals, essential fatty acids, protein, fiber—and *energy*. The body does not store carbohydrates as body fat the way it does excess dietary fat. The body "burns" the carbohydrates we eat and *stores* excess fat. It takes more energy for the body to burn fat than it does to burn carbohydrates, so fat is stored and carbohydrates are used.

Excess stored fat in the body is not serving you in any way. It is not energizing, vitalizing, or feeding your cells, organs, or bones. The old myth about fat padding our bodies against harm is ridiculous. It pads the arteries, and it can kill us.

The All-New Free to Be Thin lifestyle plan is one of energy and vitality. Your daily menu utilizing complex carbohydrates and minimizing fat will produce results. Countless success stories will attest to this.

Carbohydrates are the main source of the body's energy. During digestion, starches and sugars—the principal kinds of carbohydrates—are broken down into glucose, better known as blood sugar. This blood sugar provides vital energy for your brain and central nervous system. Gram for gram, carbohydrates have the same calories as protein.

THE TRUTH ABOUT CHOLESTEROL

What is *cholesterol*?

We all know cholesterol is one of the major risk factors in blood vascular diseases. Cholesterol and several other factors are associated with fat (lipid) buildup on the inner wall of the arteries. The fat actually perforates the wall of the artery, causing an arteriole injury. Through a calcium reaction, placque is formed.

This placque is a combination of fat, cholesterol, fiber, and calcium. It narrows the arteriole openings and increases blood pressure while it decreases the blood flow.

Cholesterol is indeed linked with heart disease, and the media is full of warnings about cholesterol in the diet. Cholesterol, combining to form placque on the arteries, narrows them, and a resulting disease called arteriosclerosis causes 850,000 deaths a year. We need to be aware of cholesterol!

Not all cholesterol is bad, though. At least two-thirds of your body cholesterol is produced by the liver or in the intestines. It is also found in the brain, the adrenals, and the nerve fiber sheaths. Lipotropics have as their main function the prevention of abnormal or excessive fat accumulation in the liver. Lipotropics increase the liver's production of lecithin, which keeps cholesterol more soluble, detoxifies the liver, and increases resistance to disease. The two most common are the low-density lipoproteins (LDL) and the high-density lipoproteins (HDL). These molecules are directly linked to the transport of cholesterol once absorbed within the body.

LDL CHOLESTEROL LEVELS	
(milligrams of cholesterol per deciliter of blood)	
Below 200	Desirable
Between 200 and 239	Borderline
240 and above	High
If your cholesterol level is 240 mg/dl or higher, your risk of heart disease is unacceptably high.	

The LDL molecules are the undesirable ones. They carry cholesterol into the system, depositing a fatty substance or residue in the arterial walls. The HDL molecules are the good ones, and remove cholesterol from the system. HDL molecules interfere with the binding of LDL-cholesterol to the cell membrane. They've also been found to remove cholesterol placque that has already been deposited in the arterial walls. HDL molecules are composed primarily of lecithin, which breaks up cholesterol and can transport it easily through the blood without clogging arteries. The higher your level of HDL, the lower your chances of developing symptoms of heart disease.

WHAT ABOUT CHOLESTEROL-FREE FOODS?

A cholesterol-free food can still be high in fat. Remember, cholesterol buildup is caused by high intake of fat. Many factors, including genetics, determine how much cholesterol remains in our bloodstreams from the foods we eat. Some people can eat a high-cholesterol diet and still have low blood cholesterol levels.

The important thing is to be more aware of *saturated fat*, which means *meat* and *whole dairy products*. Saturated fat prevents the body from removing bad cholesterol from the blood. When you focus on cholesterol instead of saturated fat, you will be misguided. Foods that are high in saturated fats are meats, including sausage, salami, and bacon; shortening, coconut and palm oil; and whole-milk dairy products.

To be healthier, you must consume less fat. A cholesterol-free food can still be high in fat. Products such as corn chips or potato chips may be advertised as containing no cholesterol, but these foods are *not* fat-free. Remember, only animal products contain cholesterol. Vegetable oil may not have cholesterol, but it is still oil. You may be surprised to know that potato chips have nearly 100 percent of their calories from fat. The Food and Drug Administration has passed regulations that will require manufacturers to list fat content immediately after any cholesterol claims on a high-fat food. It is important to read labels!

Fat cannot be converted into muscle through exercise, but regular exercise—such as walking, running, swimming, rowing, cycling, and step workouts—can reduce fat. Aerobic exercise uses stored fat as fuel, but coupled with proper diet it will greatly alter your body composition. Exercise also lowers your cholesterol level.

HOW ABOUT PROTEIN?

In the past we were taught that the more protein in our diet, the healthier we'd be. We used to think protein was the foundation of every meal. The rest of our food simply complemented large amounts of protein. Now we know that too much protein is actually detrimental to our health, and we fare better with much less than previously believed.

The days when we consumed large portions of eggs, cheese, milk, yogurt, red meat, fish, and poultry into our three meals are over. We thought of protein as the body's cure-all and build-all. We drank protein drinks, chewed protein wafers and snacked on cheese and soybean preparations. Rarely did we consider getting our protein from vegetable sources.

Your body needs protein. You couldn't digest food without it. Your bones, skin, nerves, hair, blood vessels, muscles, cartilage, lymph, hormones, enzymes, and antibodies all contain protein. Protein is necessary in every part of the body. *But* you don't need huge quantities of it. In fact, surplus protein not used by the body for energy or repair is stored as fat.

The Recommended Dietary Allowance for protein is .8 grams for 2.2 pounds of body weight for adults, or *44 grams of protein a day for the average woman and 56 grams for the average man.* That's only 10 to 15 percent of your daily calorie intake. Women who are losing weight need no more than 6 ounces of meat a day.

We are eating too much protein! Not only that, but our primary source is fatty animal protein such as red meat, cheeses, and whole milk. Too much animal protein builds our blood-level of excess fat and cholesterol, increasing the risk of several chronic diseases such as cancer of the breast, colon, and rectum.

How are you getting your protein? If you think a juicy chuck steak is providing a healthy dose of protein, think again. About 66 percent of that steak is *saturated* fat, more than half! Cheddar cheese is 74 percent *saturated* fat!

YOUR BEST SOURCES OF PROTEIN

Plant foods—that is, fruits, grains, and vegetables—contain a combination of protein, fats, and carbohydrates. Foods such as legumes and grains contain all the essential amino acids for protein to satisfy your daily requirements. When eaten in sufficient quantities and varieties, all combinations of plant foods, including vegetables, legumes, grains, and fruits, contain the nine essential amino acids that the body cannot make on its own. (There are a total of 23 essential amino acids.) Lean meats, poultry without the skin, skim milk products, and fish are also protein foods.

FREE TO BE THIN EATING FOR LIFE

We are learning how to *eat,* not how to diet.

We are learning how to *eat,* and because of it, we will be healthier, and we *will lose weight.*

We are learning how to *eat,* and that is why our new lifestyle is not just for a couple of weeks, months, or even years, but for the rest of our lives.

Now is the time to evaluate your current ideas of good health. Just how healthy has your diet been? What kind of protein have you been eating, and how much? How much and what kind of fat have you been putting into your body? What about the carbohydrates? Are you eating mainly nutritious complex carbohydrates or the unhealthy refined kind?

Take time now to answer the following:

1. Am I willing to examine my eating habits and change those that have been hurting my precious body?
2. Am I willing to keep an account of my fat, protein, and carbohydrate intake?
3. Am I willing to try new foods that will bless my precious body?
4. Am I willing to be healthier and feel more energetic?
5. Am I willing to be kind to myself and treat myself with loving respect?
6. Here are four ways I will be kind to myself and treat myself with loving respect:

- _____

- _____

- _____

- _____

In all these things we are more than conquerors through him who loved us. (Romans 8:37)

PRAYER

Lord Jesus, thank you for making me more than a conqueror. I will conquer my old bad habits. I will take a penetrating and honest look at my daily life pattern in order to see where I've been consuming too much fat and an abundance of refined carbohydrates and animal proteins.

I will allow myself to change, because it is the loving thing to do. I will allow myself to be kind and treat myself with respect. I will conquer because you love me and formed the path of victory for me to take. In your name. Amen.

8

THE ALL-NEW FREE TO BE THIN LIFESTYLE FITNESS PLAN

Are you one of these people who shrink from the very word "fitness"?

Physical fitness does *not* have to be tedious work! You do not have to be worn out, miserable, aching, and hobbling around in pain after exercising. Deborah Szekely Mazzanti, founder of the famous spa The Golden Door, once said, "Exercise can be dull; therefore I must help make it irresistible." That's what we want to do—make your exercise program irresistible!

The All-New Free to Be Thin lifestyle fitness plan is actually *more* than enjoyable. It has changed our lives and given us an inner thrill that has gone deeper than happiness. At this beginning point, ask yourself these questions:

- *Do I want to be healthy?*
- *Can I commit myself to being healthy?*

The All-New Free to Be Thin lifestyle plan is committed to your *health.* For too long our physical selves have been disassociated from our spiritual selves and we are hurting because of it. Your body—His temple—needs to be kept in good working order. Your life was meant to be lived abundantly. What is it you would like the Lord to help you accomplish? Check below:

I want . . .
- ☐ more energy
- ☐ a happier disposition
- ☐ a stronger body
- ☐ greater stamina
- ☐ healthier skin

☐ better muscle tone
☐ vibrant appearance
☐ new vitality for the rest of my life

"Not by might nor by power, but by my Spirit," says the Lord Almighty. (Zechariah 4:6)

This Bible verse can become real to you as you begin to get your body into shape. You can tell by the points you just checked above that your body needs some loving attention. You are in charge of your body. Nobody else is.

FAMOUS EXCUSES AND THE WRONG SOLUTIONS

Do you recognize any of these excuses for staying lazy and out of shape?

Excuse	*Solution*
I'm nervous	eat something
I'm worried	eat some more
I'm angry	eat something crunchy, go out for fast food
I'm anxious	never be without something to eat nearby; snack after meals
I'm lonely	eat enough for two—or three, or more
I'm fearful	take your cookies with you in the car, and always have something to eat at your bedside.

We're not trying to pry—but haven't you excused your food and body abuse with things like loneliness or emotional trauma? Carolyn once spent the entire evening sitting at her kitchen counter eating cheese and crackers and drinking diet soda while telling herself that nobody would ever love her because she was too fat.

Nobody likes to be lonely. But when you are overwhelmed with loneliness, self-pity can become a roaring giant within you. Instead of dealing with the loneliness, you may make choices that are destructive—overeating, not exercising, running away from life, or choosing situations that will abuse your integrity. *These are not God's answer to loneliness.* Because you have tried to cope in the past by overeating, you will be tempted to eat whenever you allow yourself to indulge in self-pity. Remember, self-pity can try to visit, but you don't have to open the door and let it in.

Call it any name you will, but an excuse is still an *excuse.* The reason we get out of shape is that we make excuses not to exercise, like:

- I'm too busy.
- I'm sick.
- I can't afford the workout clothes.
- I don't have enough room where I live.
- I don't want to ruin my hair and nails. (Don't let them ruin *you.*)
- My husband likes me the way I am. (Unhealthy? You want to bet?)
- I don't want to get muscular like those female body-builders. (Don't worry. Body building is a dedicated full-time career.)
- Exercise is tiresome. (Sickness is more tiresome.)

WHY THIS PROGRAM IS DIFFERENT FROM ANY OTHER FITNESS PROGRAM YOU'VE TRIED BEFORE

Here is the secret: *It is the inner person we are really developing here.* Your outside will show it, but your inner person is the one who really benefits.

> *I pray that out of his glorious riches he may strengthen you with power through his Spirit in your inner being.* (Ephesians 3:16)

When we read the words "And do not grieve the Holy Spirit of God, with whom you were sealed for the day of redemption" (Ephesians 4:30), we cannot overlook our bodies, which are the temple of the Holy Spirit. How unfortunate if we do not allow Him to fully use His own temple! Maybe He has your heart, your thoughts, your good deeds—but your poor body is in sad shape. Is the temple of the Holy Spirit getting weak at every seam?

We want you to see that *The All-New Free to Be Thin* lifestyle plan is a spiritual endeavor. The Bible tells us to exercise ourselves unto godliness:

> *For physical training is of some value, but godliness has*

*value for all things, holding promise for both the present life
and the life to come.* (1 Timothy 4:8)

We train ourselves to be stronger physically, just as we train ourselves to be stronger spiritually. We know we have the Lord's total approval, and it is a great joy to be able to develop the stamina needed to carry out His work—to serve Him more effectively. We train our bodies as well as our minds because of our love for Him.

BECOMING STRONG

Your goal, then, is to be strong inside in order to shine outside. Of course it's a waste of time to try to accomplish this without the Lord's help. We have seen weight loss and exercise programs topple because pride and vanity have been the primary motivators. The root problem of self-inflicted body abuse was never tackled. We are overcoming more than our food and body abuse. We are overcoming our drive to hurt ourselves.

Remember: Pride is a killer—it's the devil's chief weapon. He wants you to become obsessed with your body in order to keep your mind off God. We want you to decide right now before turning another page of this book that you are going to engage in this program because you want to experience God more fully, with a life dedicated to physical health and fitness as well as a healthy spiritual commitment.

"Your attitude should be the same as that of Christ Jesus," the apostle Paul wrote in Philippians 2:5. Practice having the same attitude Jesus had—one of humble submission—and let that attitude affect how you treat your body.

In the hundreds of seminars, workshops, retreats, and meetings we have led all across the United States and in other countries, we are asked to pray for the sick. When people come to us at the end of the meetings or services, no matter where we are, at least one-third of the people request prayer for physical healing. Why is this?

Let me ask this question a different way: Do you pray for your body when it is healthy and well? Or do you only pray for it when you are sick and need healing? For those struggling with being overweight, our guess is that your body is, overall, the most neglected part of you.

No longer do you need be a victim of sickness, weakness,

lethargy, depression, sloth, and lackluster living.

Being out of shape and staying that way can be a form of pride. But how can that be true?

"God loves me as I am" can mask an attitude that really says, "I'm not about to change."

Yes, He loves you, but you might feel better about loving Him back if you felt better physically. You might have more energy for life and for others.

Decide now to change your lifestyle for the sake of your body. Your mind was given to you so you could use it to make godly choices for yourself in your world. Use it now to choose God's plan for health and fitness.

I choose to reach toward my full potential as the person God created me to be. I choose to give the Lord my body so the Holy Spirit can live in a clean, healthy temple; therefore, I can live my life glorifying Him as a healthier, happier person. I choose to love and bless my body. I will not be afraid to exercise.

YOUR BEAUTIFUL BODY AND HOW IT WORKS

Take a moment now to understand your body. There are approximately 660 muscles and 208 bones in your body. Just think how happy they'll be now that you're going to give them some attention. After all, they deserve a little fun in life, too!

Your miraculous blood: Your body has sixty thousand miles of blood vessels if you're a woman, and seventy-five thousand if you're a man. This life flow within you carries oxygen, water, nutrients, hormones, protective antibodies, and dozens of other vital substances to each of your 60 trillion cells. Your blood repairs biological damage, gets rid of cellular waste, and works overtime when you're sick.

Your marvelous heart: That magnificent heart of yours, with its four-chambered muscular pump, moves blood through your lungs and into your blood vessels. That wonderful instrument of life in your body beats *more than 36 million times a year.* For all that work, don't you think it deserves some loving care? It works all day and night for you without stopping.

Your heart actually doesn't work as well if you don't give it something to do. It's a muscle, after all. A person who is in top physical condition by exercising regularly will have a resting heart rate of about sixty beats per minute or less. A person who is not in good condition forces the heart to beat nearly 30,000 times more every day of his or her life. If you are out of shape, your heart will beat proportionately faster than if you were in shape doing the same activity. And if your heart is not in shape, the rest of you is not in shape, either.

Dr. Kenneth Cooper, the father of aerobics, has a good illustration describing your heart and how it works. He says the heart is like a "lawn with built-in watering jets, or like one watered with a small garden hose. The hose might water the entire lawn eventually but, during a hot spell, it might take too long and some of the lawn might burn up. If part of your heart 'burned up' because it couldn't get enough sprinkling, it could mean a heart attack."

Oxygen: The key to a healthy heart, lungs, and cardiovascular system is oxygen. The body can store food, but it can't store oxygen. The body uses the food it wants and stores the rest, but oxygen has to be constantly replenished in our bodies. The blood *needs* oxygen. When you exercise, you are pumping more blood and increasing the efficiency of your heart. You increase the number and size of the blood vessels that carry the blood to your body tissue, saturating the tissues throughout your whole body with energy-producing oxygen. Exercise will increase your total blood volume and improve the tone of your blood vessels, often reducing blood pressure in the process. In other words, *you can win your war with fat and cholesterol with your new exercise program*!

Your blood pressure and pulse: These are two of the most important indicators of the condition of your circulatory system. That's why the doctor checks them first. Every time your heart contracts or beats, it pumps your blood to all points of your body. When you place your fingertips lightly on your pulse points, you can feel your pulse as your blood moves through your arteries with each contraction. The slower the pulse rate, the more efficiently your heart is beating. In other words, your heart is sending out more blood with fewer contractions per minute.

The average person's heart beats about 70 times a minute when at rest. There are some super athletes with much lower resting pulse rates. A tennis pro we know, for instance, has a resting heart rate of only 36!

Blood pressure is the force of your blood against the walls of the vessels as it flows merrily through. It is recorded as two numbers, one written over the other—for example, 120/80. The top, or *systolic,* number is the pressure occurring in the blood vessels when your heart contracts. The bottom, or *diastolic,* number is the minimum pressure in the vessels as your heart rests between contractions.

You should be aware of your blood pressure rate and have it checked about once a year. Most specialists agree that 120/80 is a good average pressure, though this will vary a bit for each person.

When you are out of condition, both your systolic and your diastolic figures are relatively higher because your arteries tend to lose their elasticity and the resistance to blood flow increases. Certain factors can temporarily raise your normal blood pressure. James J. Lynch, Ph.D., professor of psychophysiology at the University of Maryland School of Medicine, discovered that even talking can raise blood pressure. He tested six hundred people of all ages, and almost without exception, blood pressure rose 10 to 50 percent when adults talked, babies cried, deaf people used sign language, and when people read aloud to themselves.

You have a problem if your blood pressure becomes high too often or stays up too long. Or if it bounces up and down like a yo-yo, or takes too long to come down after being high, you could have a problem. Hypertension affects 18 million American women a year.

Some other factors putting you at risk for high blood pressure are oral contraceptives, pregnancy, and menopause, according to cardiologist Harriet Dustean, M.D., formerly president of the American Heart Association. Don't panic if you have high blood pressure. Dr. Lewis Tobian, an expert on hypertensive therapy at the University of Minnesota Medical Center, says, "The combination of *proper diet* [one that is lower in sodium and in calories for the overweight] and appropriate medication can lower the blood pressure to normal levels in virtually every hypertensive person."

At one time, the treatment of high blood pressure was rest and relaxation because hypertension was associated with stress. Now, physicians insist upon regular exercise to neutralize unavoidable daily stress. In your new exercise program, you will improve the blood supply to your heart, which also keeps the surrounding heart tissue healthy. When fat circulates in your bloodstream for prolonged periods, the length of time it takes to get rid of it depends on you. If you are in good physical condition, your body will get rid of the fat more quickly.

Take this moment to commit even your blood system to God.

PRAYER

Father, I ask you to bless my blood system now in the name of Jesus Christ—my blood pressure, my blood chemistry, my blood count. The Word of God tells me it is the Spirit who gives life, and therefore I give my entire self to you. And I trust in your Word, which says, "And if the Spirit of him who raised Jesus from the dead is living in you, he who raised Christ from the dead will also give life to your mortal bodies through his Spirit, who lives in you" (Romans 8:11).

9

The Lifetime Benefits of Your All-New Free to Be Thin Lifestyle Fitness Plan

A Fitness Test

Did you know these facts?

- The physically fit person is able to withstand fatigue for longer periods than the unfit.
- The physically fit person is better equipped to tolerate physical stress.
- The physically fit person has a stronger and more efficient heart.
- There is a relationship between good mental alertness, absence of nervous tension, and physical fitness.

With these in mind, answer the following questions with as much honesty as you can:

1. At Christmas and other holidays, I make excuses for overeating and find it difficult to return to my eating plan. ☐ True ☐ False
2. When I finish the food on my plate, I pick food off someone else's plate. ☐ True ☐ False
3. When I carry heavy items like groceries or suitcases, I feel winded and out of breath. ☐ True ☐ False
4. Sometimes I wear a coat or baggy clothes even in warm weather to hide my body. ☐ True ☐ False

5. I always look for a parking place nearest   ☐ True   ☐ False
   the entrance of the supermarket so I
   don't have to walk far.
6. I'm convinced that most movie stars   ☐ True   ☐ False
   have beautiful figures, not because they
   exercise but because they were either
   born that way or they have had exten-
   sive plastic surgery.
7. I'd rather go to a new restaurant even if   ☐ True   ☐ False
   I'm not hungry than go for a brisk walk
   or learn a new sport such as tennis or
   low-impact aerobics.

Scoring: Give yourself two points for each question you answered "False."

> 12–14 points: Fabulous! You are exemplary.
> 8–12 points: Aren't you glad you are now on *The All-New
>   Free to Be Thin* lifestyle plan? You will benefit
>   greatly!
> 6 and under: Don't delay. Use *The All-New Free to Be Thin*
>   lifestyle plan to start making changes in your
>   life now!

A BEAUTIFUL TODAY WITH AEROBIC EXERCISE

Familiarize yourself now with the following information
about exercise. Aerobic exercises are activities such as fast walking, running, low-impact aerobics, step workouts, bicycling, and
swimming that stimulate heart and lung activity for an extended
period of time to produce significant changes in your body. With
aerobic exercise, your lungs, heart, and vascular system all benefit, as well as your muscles and bones.

Aerobic means "with oxygen." Aerobic exercise requires oxygen and causes your cardiovascular and respiratory system—
your heart, lungs, and blood vessels—to operate more efficiently.
They are better able to take oxygen from the air, process it, and
deliver it to your muscles and organs. When you're in shape,
your cardiorespiratory system has less work to do in order to
keep your body running well.

Your heart is going to love you for your new getting-in-shape
program. You're going to breathe easier because the muscles in

your chest will grow stronger, and you will be able to breathe air in and out of your lungs with less effort.

You will reduce your risk of heart disease, heart attack, and stroke. You don't have to be a marathon runner to achieve these excellent results. Any increase in your level of physical activity will make you more fit. It doesn't matter what shape you're in now, how old you are, or how long it's been since you were physically active. Anyone can be fit, have a healthier heart, and bless her or his body. Please be sure to consult with your physician before you engage in any physical fitness program. Listen to his or her advice and counsel.

To get the most from your aerobic exercise program, it must include the following important components.[1]

- *Frequency of Exercise:* A minimum of three days per week, preferably on alternate days. Maximum: six days a week. Your body needs one day to rest.
- *Intensity of Exercise:* You will want to reach 60 to 80 percent of your projected maximal heart rate. Your maximal heart rate per minute during aerobic exercise is approximately 200 minus your age.
- *Time:* Twenty to thirty minutes spent in continuous, steady aerobic conditioning. This can be worked into slowly, building up the time of each exercise period with five-minute increases as you are able.
- *Type of Exercise:* You will be doing exercises and aerobic activities that work your heart and lungs as well as utilize the muscle groups in your arms, legs, back, and abdomen.

ARE YOU BREATHING?

Of course you're breathing, or you wouldn't be reading this book. The important matter, though, is this: Are you breathing *correctly?* The way you breathe makes a big difference. Shallow breathing brings only a portion of your lung cells into play, and your body is thus under-oxygenated.

Give yourself this little test: Stand up and take a deep breath. As you breathe, are your shoulders raised and your breath up at the base of your throat? If so, you are breathing shallow. Not good.

---

[1]Dr. Frank Katch, University of Massachusetts.

AEROBIC ACTIVITIES AND THEIR BENEFITS	
High- and Low-Impact Aerobic Exercise	Benefits
Brisk Walking:	Great choice for almost everyone. Keep a good fast pace for best cardiovascular benefits. Burns fat, builds strength and endurance.
Jogging:	Excellent cardiovascular, muscular, and all-around body workout. Burns fat, builds strength and endurance.
Swimming:	Best cardiovascular conditioning exercise there is. No twisted ankles or blisters. Exercises all muscle groups and instead of muscle bulk, builds long, lean muscles. A vigorous swim will burn as many as five hundred calories in half an hour.
Skipping Rope:	Develops and strengthens calves, shoulder muscles, and forearms. Tones quadriceps, hamstring, abdominal, pectoral, upper back, and bicep muscles. Good overall aerobic workout.
Rebound Jumping:	Improves the heart and lungs and strengthens legs.
Cross-country Skiing:	Arm, shoulder, waist, abdomen, buttocks, calf, and ankle muscles strengthened. One of the best cardiovascular workouts.
Bicycling:	Strengthens and tones thighs, calves, forearms, and buttocks. Heart and lungs work more efficiently; circulation is improved.
High- and Low-Impact Aerobic Classes:	A top workout, which always includes warm-up and cool-down. Three to six one-hour low-impact classes a week will bring amazing results. Overall fitness.

Another way of breathing incorrectly is to puff out your chest as you take in breath. You are using only about half your lung's capacity when you breathe this way.

The correct way to breathe is to use your diaphragm, the muscle covering the abdomen in an arc and protruding into your chest cavity. Your diaphragm will expand when your lower lungs are filled. In correct deep breathing, your stomach will appear to swell. This is giving your lungs an "air bath"!

Try another breath now, this time with your hands on your stomach. Take a deep breath and feel your stomach expand. If you practice this often, you will be filling your lungs and raising the oxygen level of your blood to an energetic high point. You will also be aiding in the expulsion of toxins and wastes.

Breathing properly is essential to your health because your cells need oxygen. Oxygen combined with glucose (or the body's fuel) in your bloodstream forms energy. Anything you do that interferes with your body's processes of oxygenation and the removal of carbon dioxide will cause your cells to slowly become exhausted.

Exercise is vital to your respiration. The oxygen capacity of your lungs increases with exercise, and stored fat is used up. Always, always take several deep breaths during your exercise time, as you warm up and cool down. Breathe evenly as you exercise.

WHY AEROBIC EXERCISE?

Aerobic exercise is the basis of your *All-New Free to Be Thin* lifestyle fitness plan. It will produce the results you need. You can choose from high-impact and low-impact aerobic exercise, swimming, running, walking, rowing, cycling, a treadmill, stairmaster, cross-country skiing, and other creative workouts such as kick boxing, step classes, and making use of the many excellent pieces of sports equipment designed for cardiovascular workouts.

Aerobic exercise will strengthen your cardiovascular system, lower your resting pulse rate, keep your body-fat percentage at lower levels, tone muscles, and burn calories. These exercises cannot be performed at a minimum level of exertion if they are to benefit you fully. Jogging lazily or paddling around in a pool without effort will not give you an optimum pulse rate. To be aerobically fit, you need to do your daily workout nonstop for at least 15 to 20 minutes.

> *Praise the Lord, O my soul; all my inmost being, praise his holy name. Praise the Lord, O my soul, and forget not all his benefits.* (Psalm 103:1–2)

The Lord has given you many benefits because you belong to Him. He not only forgives your sins but He heals your diseases as well (Isaiah 53 and Psalm 103). He redeems your life from destruction. He crowns you with lovingkindness and tender mercies. He will satisfy you with good things and renew your youth like the eagle's (Psalm 103:3–5).

Let's look at some of the ways your health can be improved.

EXERCISE IS VITAL

You will be amazed to learn how many physical problems can be relieved or eliminated with exercise. Some are:

Headache: There are countless studies showing that headaches and tension problems that elevate blood pressure and place huge overloads on your circulatory system can be relieved by exercises.

Isn't that great news? Instead of reaching for the aspirin, reach for your aerobics shoes and start your workout!

As you begin exercising, you will feel your body relaxing and tension headaches lifting. The reason for this relief is a result of vasodilation (enlargement of the blood vessels). The increased size of the blood vessels allows a lowering of blood pressure as well as an increase in the amount of oxygen to the brain.

Pain in the neck (And we don't mean your in-laws!): This includes pinched nerves, thoracic outlet syndrome, and other disorders. You will be given specific exercises for your upper body. Do them faithfully every day for best results.

Backaches: A common reason for back pain is not using your abdominal muscles. The abdominal muscles help support the back, alleviating excess pressure or stress on the back muscles.

Poor posture, faulty positions of standing and sitting, improper rising, and unbalanced carrying of heavy loads can contribute to back problems. Spinal curvatures such as *kyphosis, lordosis,* and *scoliosis* need to be specially treated by a physician. If you are like most of us, however, your backaches are probably due to poor posture, faulty positions of standing and sitting, and lack of muscular support.

Slouching, slumping, and sitting hunched over produces stress and strain on your spinal column. It will rebel with aches and pains.

If you lead a sedentary life, how much more do you need to exercise those muscles of yours to support your body properly! If you sit most of the day, you will, among other things, develop abdominal muscle deterioration unless it is counteracted by appropriate exercise.

Other maladies such as varicose veins, constipation, joint stiffness, edema, and general malaise will all be helped by exercise. Marilyn learned the fun and benefits of aerobic activity when she began to play tennis again. Then she was in a devastating car accident, and doctors told her that chances of her ever playing tennis again were slim. She exercised and worked hard building her strength. In five months she was playing tennis, and even went on to win a championship through her tennis club competition. She says, "I believe God used tennis in my life to bring a healing to my body as well as my mind. After my accident I was miserable. All those broken bones. My right hand was paralyzed. I lay in bed all day feeling sorry for myself."

Marilyn radiated enthusiasm as she continued: "I decided to stop feeling sorry for myself. Instead I prayed for strength. I wanted to play tennis again and I prayed God would give me the inner strength to work toward that goal. He answered my prayer! I can honestly say now I've never felt better in my life. Winning the tennis championship was like a gift from the Lord. It was He saying to me, 'We made it!' "

Marilyn made it, and so will you. And you will have fun as you do it.

In conclusion, the facts are simple. You absolutely *must* include daily exercise in your life. Do not wait. Do it *now*. Tell yourself you are a physically active person from now on.

PRAYER

Dear Jesus, thank you for the strength to be more than I have the ability to be. Thank you for your power and your love that breathes life and vigor into my whole being. Thank you for repairing me and lifting me out of the doldrums of self-centeredness. Thank you for fitness, and thank you for loving me. Thank you for the gift of exercise. Amen.

10

Your Choice to Be Fit

Joys of Exercise

Decide now. You have no choice when it comes to exercise. You do it. It is an important part of your daily routine. Period. Now, let's look at the exercises that are just right for your body.

Do you know the types of exercises that give your body best results? There are five basic exercise categories.

Aerobics: As we learned in chapter nine, aerobic exercise stimulates the cardiovascular system for an extended period of time to produce significant changes in the body. We have already discussed some of the benefits of aerobic exercise.

Some exercises do not show any appreciable health benefit, but they can complement an aerobic exercise routine or program. These exercises are aimed at strengthening the skeletal muscles and make no demands on your lungs, heart, and blood system. They are:

Isometrics: These exercises involve contracting a muscle without producing movement. For example, you place your palms on either side of your doorway and press for a few seconds. This kind of exercise strengthens and tones muscles.

Isometric exercises can increase the size and strength of your skeletal muscles, and are especially good when you are sitting for long periods of time. Secretaries, accountants, writers, and other demanding yet sedentary occupations can benefit from isometric breaks, and isometrics are good for bedridden patients. But isometrics work on only one muscle group at a time, and it would take a long time to use all of your muscles. These exercises do not demand oxygen and are primarily for strengthening muscles.

Isotonics: Isotonic means "equal tension." Isotonics are basically muscle exercises, calisthenics and weight lifting. These exercises are good for your body, but they are not enough by themselves to produce optimum physical fitness. Calisthenics are valuable, but they should not be considered the *foundation* of any exercise program. They will develop your muscles, slim you down, and build you up, but they will not affect your heart and lungs significantly. *The All-New Free to Be Thin* lifestyle fitness plan includes isotonics because they work to strengthen and tone your muscles. Weight training will increase your muscular strength and endurance, as well as improve your flexibility especially when combined with stretching.

Isokinetics: These exercises are performed on machines and help strengthen and tone many different muscle groups. One of the best-known brands of isokinetic machines is the Nautilus line of weight-lifting machines. These machines allow a muscle group to meet resistance through movement. You work your body in a variety of positions as you move weights attached to pulleys and rotary cams. Some exercise equipment offers stations at which you can work up to twelve or more different muscle groups. Many of these machines are also available for home use.

Anaerobics: The term *anaerobic* means "without oxygen." These exercises do not require oxygen and are short-duration, high-intensity activities. An example of anaerobic exercise is running the one-hundred-yard dash. This type of exercise rapidly creates large oxygen debts, but does not include a warm-up, steady pace, or cool-down period. In order to increase your level of cardiovascular fitness, you need to do exercises that demand oxygen for an *extended, steady period of time.*

YOUR CHOICE TO BE FIT

The definition of physical fitness, according to the *Physical Fitness Research Digest* published by the President's Council on Physical Fitness and Sports, is "the ability to carry out daily tasks with vigor and alertness, without undue tiredness, and with ample energy to enjoy leisure-time pursuits and to meet unusual situations and unforeseen emergencies." We can safely say, then, that physical fitness gives you the ability to live at your utmost level of health and vitality. Fitness enables you to be mentally, emotionally, and physically alert and sound. The more fit you are, the better your quality of life.

The words "Therefore do not let sin reign in your mortal body" (Romans 6:12) mean that we need to decide *who* is Lord over our bodies. We often think serving the Lord has nothing to do with being healthy or physically fit. Paul writes in Romans 12:1 that we are to present our bodies a living sacrifice, holy and pleasing to God, and that is our reasonable service. God teaches us that it is only right and natural that we should present our bodies to Him, that we might be in top shape ready for His use.

If you were to hire somebody to work for you in your company, would you choose the one who is glowing with health, energy, and strength, or would you choose the one who moves slowly, with difficulty, and tires quickly? Though both employees may be qualified and dedicated to you and the company, which one would be of the most service to you?

You are a person fit for the Master's use now. Say it out loud: "In Him, I am complete."

Jesus said that He came to give you *life* and to give it to you more abundantly (John 10:10). As Christians, we are privileged to have an abundance of God's life in us. The Greek word *zoe,* found in the New Testament 130 times, means "life." This life is God's own life, and you can have His life as a gift from Him.

The life of God lives within you when you are filled with His Spirit. Even if you think you could never be physically fit, you can grasp the words "Everything is possible for him who believes" (Mark 9:23). You are filled with God's own life. You have the privilege of a full and abundant life and can expect to be complete in Christ (Colossians 2:10).

Through the life of God within you, you are made more than a conqueror—spirit, soul, and body.

THE FOOD OF LIFE

Here are some Bible verses to meditate on as you exercise, and throughout the day. Make God's powerful promises personal:

God instructs me and teaches me the way I should go. He councils me with His eye upon me. (See Psalm 32:8–9.)

Nothing separates me from the love of Christ. Not tribulation, distress, persecution, famine, nakedness, peril or sword. (See Romans 8:35–39.)

This I know, that you are pleased with me. (See Psalm 41:11.)

I am strong and of good courage. I am not frightened or dismayed, for the Lord, my God, is with me wherever I go. (See Joshua 1:9.)

When I pass through the waters the Lord is with me; and through the rivers, they shall not overwhelm me; when I walk through the fire, I shall not be burned, neither shall the flames set me ablaze. (See Isaiah 43:2.)

I will not let my heart be troubled. I trust in God and I trust in the Lord Jesus Christ. In my Father's house are many mansions; if it were not so, the Lord would have told me. (See John 14:1–2.)

All things are possible to me because I believe. (See Mark 9:23.)

I submit myself to God. I resist the devil and he flees from me. (See James 4:7.)

This is His Word—and this is where our new strength begins. We have our feet solidly placed on a firm foundation.

11

KNOWING YOUR WONDERFUL MUSCLES

God gave you your muscles to use them, develop them, and be strong in order to live a good life. Muscles are contractile tissues composed of fibrils, which shorten when chemically activated. Your muscles comprise 35 to 45 percent of your total body weight (remember that when you get on the scale).

WHY SOME OF YOUR BEST FRIENDS ARE YOUR MUSCLES

In order to understand your body and why *The All-New Free to Be Thin* lifestyle plan stresses exercise, we want you to take the time to learn about your muscles and how they work.

You have three kinds of muscles:

Skeletal: under voluntary control (these are the ones you work);

Cardiac: found only in the heart;

Smooth: as in the intestine (involuntary and controlled by the autonomic nervous system).

Now, here's what happens when you exercise. Your skeletal muscles are designed to contract, and as they do, they are strengthened. Muscle tone is maintained when your fibrils are regularly stimulated to contract.

Muscles come in pairs, like brother and sister, so that as one contracts, the other slowly relaxes for a smooth, controlled movement. Toned muscles pull gently against each other, looking and feeling resilient.

Here's the best part: When your muscles contract, energy is required and heat is produced. This makes a change in metabolism and produces carbon dioxide, lactic acid, heat, and water. The blood flow into the muscles is increased to take away metabolites, the products of metabolism, and your heart rate increases. Your body works to cool itself with perspiration.

What it all means is that when you exercise, you make your muscles very happy and, after all, what are friends for?

You have more than *434 skeletal muscles* responsible for every move you make. When you successfully stimulate fitness in the large-muscle groups, your minor-muscle groups are affected in the process. There are fifteen basic muscle groups, and when you give them a thorough workout, most of the 434 skeletal muscles will benefit.

For most of the actions your body performs, your muscles are working together in order to do what you want them to. Most muscles have more than one function. When you are just sitting or standing, your muscles are constantly contracting (shortening) and extending (lengthening) to balance your body against the forces of gravity. These movements are automatic, and you don't have to consciously think about them. Nevertheless, those muscles of yours are constantly at work for you. They need your attention, however, because without it they do not function as they ought to.

There are five muscle groups you will be concentrating on. Starting from your head to your toes, they are:

Upper-body muscles: The muscles in your upper body include your neck muscles, which are responsible for moving your head from front to back and side to side and protecting your upper spinal cord from injury. Also included in your upper-body muscles are your shoulder muscles. This important group of muscles, called "deltoids," covers your shoulders—top, sides, front and back. The deltoids are used in all your daily activities and all exercises that involve raising your arms.

Also included in this muscle group are your chest muscles, or pectoral muscles, which are located on the sides and center of your chest and underneath your breasts. When you lift, move, or push anything, you use your pectorals. Your breast tissue is supported by these muscles.

Upper-back muscles are made up of two important muscle groups: the trapezius, a triangle-shaped muscle located along the neck and shoulders and between the shoulder blades, and the latissimus dorsi, which run from the front of the shoulder across your sides to the middle of your back ("lats"). Most women have weak "lats," which is why we don't usually do well at chin-ups and rope climbing.

Arm muscles: There are three primary muscles in your arms.

The first is the triceps, located along the back of your upper arm. This muscle makes up two-thirds of your upper arm. Like the lats, triceps are usually underdeveloped in most women, and that is why we tend to get flabby in the upper-arm area. You use your triceps to lift things over your head or to extend your arms in any direction.

In the front of the upper arm is your biceps. This muscle's main purpose is to bend your elbow and is used in any lifting movement in which your arm is bent and in any pulling movement. The biceps work together with your lats and deltoids. If you want to see your biceps in all its glory, stand in front of a mirror, make a fist with your arm bent, and contract the muscle.

The third muscle is the forearm muscle, which is responsible for moving your wrist and for gripping. These muscles come in handy for playing tennis, hailing a cab, or chopping celery.

Abdominal muscles: Your abdominal muscles are located in the center and along the sides of your abdomen. These very important muscles aid in your posture, in stabilizing your torso during activity, and holding your internal organs in place. It is vital that these muscles be in shape. Countless disorders are due to lack of use of these muscles. Your abdominal muscles are used in all activities and all sports. You will be doing abdominal exercises daily in your new fitness plan.

Hip and lower-back muscles: Walking is a good way to strengthen your lower-back muscles. Like the abdominal muscles, the lower-back muscles are necessary in every one of your daily activities. They are extremely important in maintaining posture.

Leg muscles: The four muscle groups in your legs include the gluteal muscles, or the buttocks. This is an area of the body where women are likely to carry excess body fat. The gluteal muscles are the largest and strongest muscle group of your entire body and are used in leg movement. Conditioned gluteal muscles are essential for walking and running.

The muscle at the front of the thigh is the quadriceps, and it is used when squatting, climbing stairs, or bicycling. It is used to straighten your knees. People with knee joint problems often have weak quadriceps.

The muscle located along the back of your thigh is called the hamstring. The hamstring is used to bend your leg at the knee, and is important in all physical exercises. Tight hamstrings are sometimes a major cause of lower-back pain. This is especially common in people who don't exercise.

Calf muscles are located on the back of your lower legs. You use them when you stand on your toes, walk, bike, or do aerobic dance. Some women suffer from shortened, inflexible calf muscles, sometimes causing ankle pain, because of years of wearing high-heeled shoes. Your calves are vitally important in any daily activity that requires mobility.

In order to develop your muscles, you want to be sure to work *all* of the muscle groups. Most of us tend to be weaker in certain muscles than in others, and our daily activities develop strength and endurance in different areas of our bodies. If you run every day, you will have strength in your legs and cardiovascular strength, but chances are you have less strength when it comes to your upper body, and you may need to work on flexibility.

One young mother of four children told me (Marie) she got plenty of exercise during the day by running up and down stairs, doing the laundry, cooking, and taking care of her demanding family. Actually, she was not getting enough exercise, because all of her muscle groups were not being developed to their maximum. You may think you get enough exercise if your daily work is physical, but you are not. Say, for instance, you work as a waiter. Just because you are on your feet all day and moving quickly does not guarantee that you will have strength in the five muscle groups we have named. You need a balanced exercise program to be strong in all areas of your body.

After examining the parts of your body, you can certainly gain a greater insight into the joy of the Word: "Give thanks in all circumstances, for this is God's will for you in Christ Jesus" (1 Thessalonians 5:18).

Let's praise the Lord together and rejoice that we can glorify God by being strong and healthy for Him.

> *You were bought at a price. Therefore honor God with your body.* (1 Corinthians 6:20)

WORKOUT GUIDELINES

The Warm-up

Whatever aerobic or cardiovascular exercise you choose, whether it is low impact or high impact, rhythmic exercises, swimming, jogging, tennis, racquetball, rowing, or bicycling, you will need to warm up each time before you exercise. Even if your daily exercise is a 40-minute walk, warm up first. But do it *slowly* and carefully. *No* jerking or fast movements!

Warming up includes stretching and (slowly) getting your pulse rate up. Your metabolic system will get itself ready at this time for the exercises to come. The blood vessels in your muscles will expand and get ready for exercise. If a cold, tight muscle is suddenly shocked into violent contractions such as fast running with no warm-up, it can tear, pull, or strain. An injury can occur in a muscle fascia (the sheath covering the muscle), or in a tendon, ligament, cartilage, or even in a bone in the form of a stress fracture. We tell you all of this to emphasize the importance of lengthening and warming your muscle fibers, stretching and contracting them, so they can accommodate the strain of exercise.

Some fitness experts recommend walking or using the stationary bicycle *first* before the stretching warm-up. This is in order not to pull or injure muscles by jerking or yanking contracted muscles too fast. Do your stretches *slowly.*

You will be exercising each isolated group of muscles as you proceed through your program, moving from your head to your shoulders, to your arms and hands, to your rib cage, waist, hips, back, buttocks, thighs, lower legs, and feet in a logical progression. Relax and stretch easily, breathing slowly and rhythmically in your warm-up.

You will be warming up in another way, too. This is perhaps the most important warm-up of all, because it is the very heart and core of your entire fitness program. This warm-up is your spiritual warm-up: Take one scripture verse and speak it out loud as you stretch. For example, 2 Samuel 22:33: "It is God who arms me with strength."

Speak these words out loud. Hear them and believe them. As you start your exercises unto the Lord, you are blessing not only your body but your soul and spirit as well. Continue to repeat your verse throughout your entire warm-up. There is a strong principle we are stressing here, and it is the principle of scriptural meditation. Joshua 1:8 reads:

> *Do not let this Book of the Law depart from your mouth; meditate on it day and night, so that you may be careful to do everything written in it. Then you will be prosperous and successful.*

You are meditating on the Word of God as you speak it to yourself. You will find yourself becoming stronger not only physically but in every single area of your life.

We are including here some warm-up exercises for you to do. *Part 2* of your exercise program is your specific body-shaping exercises. We are including some excellent stomach, leg, hip, and arm exercises. *Part 3* of your program will be your aerobic section. Here's where you let loose and have a ball in whatever area of aerobic exercise you choose! Make sure it is vigorous and that you reach your target heart rate for a period no less than thirty minutes, which you will work up to gradually. The last section, *Part 4* of your workout, will be your cool-down, which we will cover in the following section. The cool-down will help prevent sore muscles and bring your entire system back to normal. It will consist of basically the same stretches you warmed up with. The purpose of the cool-down is to allow your pulse rate to return to normal. Never stop exercises abruptly. Try to walk leisurely the last five minutes after you have finished a brisk walk, jog, run, or any of the aerobic activities on the chart on page 68.

How to Know Your Pulse Rate

Place your index finger and your middle finger at the side of your neck under your jaw or on your wrist and count the beat of your heart for six seconds. Multiply that number by 10. If you come up with a count of 16 beats, for example, your heart rate is 16 times 10, or 160. This is an accurate indication of your peak exercise pulse rate.

A handy formula can help you know if you are exercising too intensely or not intensely enough. There are two exercise heart rates: The first is the Minimum Exercise Heart Rate, the minimum rate for improving cardiovascular fitness; the second is the Maximum Exercise Heart Rate, or the upper limit of recommended exercise intensity.

Here is the formula: Your Minimum Exercise Heart Rate is 170 minus your age. Your Maximum Exercise Heart Rate is 200 minus your age.

For example, if your age is 44 and your Minimum Exercise Heart Rate is 126, your Maximum Exercise Heart Rate would be 156. This means that you must reach a heart rate of 126 to begin improving cardiovascular fitness. Later on, as you become better conditioned, you can exercise with more intensity and a heart rate closer to 156. This is a formula that is very easy to remember and is an excellent guide, followed by virtually all fitness instructors.

In order for cardiovascular improvement to begin, you must reach your minimum heart rate while exercising. If you find your exercise sessions don't get you up to your minimum heart rate, increase the intensity with which you're doing your exercises, or the duration of them. Remember your FITT system:

F means Frequency: Work out five to six days per week.
I means Intensity: Work out at your target heart rate.
T means Time: Exercise for a minimum of thirty minutes per session. (In our program we start with 10-minute periods if you're really out of shape, and increase it gradually.)
T means Type of Exercise: You will be doing exercises and aerobic activities that will work out your heart and lungs as well as utilize the muscle groups in your arms, legs, back, and abdomen.

Pray as you exercise. Praise as you exercise. Worship God with your whole being!

PRAYER

Dear Lord, thank you for me and the body you've given me. Thank you for the opportunity to give you every fiber and tissue of my being so that being healthy will glorify you. In Jesus' name. Amen.

THE WARM-UP

Fabulous Stretch

With feet apart, lift your arms and stretch up as far as you can. Feel your ribcage lift. Then very gently reach your right arm up and over, bending the waist slightly. Repeat on the left side. As you bend, keep your knees soft, never stiff.

Shoulder Rolls

Feet apart, lift your shoulders up to your ears, then counting slowly to two with each movement, make an easy circle, front, down, back, down. Reverse the exercise. Do these exercises during the day to relieve a stiff neck and shoulders.

Head Rolls

If you have tension headaches, this is for you. Drop your head to the right for a count of two. Feel the stretch on the left side of your neck. Now roll your head to the back slowly, chin to the ceiling. Open and close your mouth twice, rotate to the left smoothly for a count of two, then continue the movement as you drop your head forward, chin to chest. Repeat.

Arm Stretches

1. Stand erect and reach your arms behind your back, clasping your hands together. Pull up very slightly, very gently. Hold for a count of ten as you stretch your shoulders back; straightening your back.

2. Standing with feet apart, soft knees, reach your right hand behind your head and with your lifted left arm, grab it beneath the elbow (never hold an arm or leg at the joint) and stretch gently, leaning slightly for an extra stretch of the waist. Repeat on other side for a count of five on each side.

3. With right arm across the chest in a straight line, grab the wrist with your left hand and gently pull, stretching the arm for a count of five. Repeat on other side.

4. Arms behind your back, loose knees and feet apart, touch or grab your fingers and hold for a count of five. Repeat on other side. Be sure to hold in the abdomen as you stretch. Breathe evenly.

Waist Stretches

Feet apart, hands clasped in front of the body with straight arms, bend the knees slightly and twist gently to the left and right, keeping the torso facing front. Feel the stretch in the waist. Do this several times and hold on each side for a count of two.

Mini-Lunge

1. This exercise is designed to prevent hyper-extension of the leg. Place weight on left foot stretching the right leg behind you. Bend the left knee and stretch the back leg and calf. Keep the back free from rounding and hold in stomach nice and tight. Hold the stretch for a count of five. Hands can be at waist or straight in front of you.

2. Now tuck in the buttocks, bend the back leg, raise the heel, and feel the stretch along the front of the thigh. The lower you bend the knee, the greater the stretch. Hold for five.

3. Now bring the back foot forward, straighten it, and with the toe up, reach your body gently forward and feel the stretch in the back of the leg. Keep the abdomen tucked in and the back straight. Hold for five and repeat the three steps and positions on the other leg. This is a small movement stretch and your technique is important. Keep it very controlled.

Quadriceps Stretch

Stand on one foot with or without holding onto something and gently lift one foot by holding the foot behind you so the heel touches the buttocks if possible. Hold for a count of five and repeat on other side, squeezing buttocks and pressing hips forward. Be careful not to overarch by letting stomach sag forward. Control the stomach.

Back, Legs, and Groin Stretch

Feet wide apart, reach forward and very gently lower your torso until your hands reach the ground. Your knees are bent, soft, not stiff. Hold the stretch for count of ten and as you do, bend your knees a little bit wider to give a better stretch. Then slowly and very gently roll up to a standing position and repeat.

THE WORK-OUT

Minimum of twenty minutes. Go at it slow and easy until you are up to forty-five minutes. This is your time to walk, jog, swim, or do the aerobic exercise of your choice. If you are walking, remember your technique. Tuck in the abdomen, walk at a brisk rate and swing your arms in a pumping fashion. Make this the most special time of day for yourself.

BODY SHAPING AND STRENGTHENING

Stomach: Fabulous Crunches

Lying on your back with knees bent, press the small of your back into the floor. Hands under the head, elbows out. Press in the abdomen and then lift the head only a few inches off the floor, just until shoulders are off the floor. To be sure you are in correct alignment, put your tongue on the roof of your mouth. Lift and lower, keeping the small of the back pressed down when you lower and the abdomen as tight as you can. Start with ten and work up to one hundred.

To add another movement to this exercise, lift one knee until foot is even with opposite knee and bend opposite elbow to meet the knee as you lift up. Do five on each side, working up to fifty. Your stomach will love you for this one. Control and keep the stomach tight.

Thighs, Buttocks: Strong Legs

With your body in an L-position as shown, legs slightly bent, knees soft, never stiff, lift the top leg no farther up than a few inches. Your technique is important here. Do not overextend. Lift and lower, but as you lower do not allow it to rest on the other foot. Repeat twenty-five times, working up to one hundred.

Then move that top leg forward across your body and repeat the lifting and lowering counting one-and-two. Feel the stretch in the buttocks and back of thigh. Carefully bend the knee back to starting position and repeat on other side. These may seem easy but they are very effective. Hold in the stomach and do not slump your back as you lift and lower the leg.

Inner-Thigh Raises

On your side and propped up on one elbow, bend knee and place your hand on it. The other leg is straight out in front of you with foot flexed and toe pointed out. Gently lift and lower this leg twenty-five times. You can also cross over the bent leg, holding the ankle and raise the straight leg. Most important is to keep that foot flexed. Repeat on both sides. Keep the stomach tight.

COOL DOWN

Breathe

Take a big breath in lifting your hands over your head and then lowering them. Feel your lungs expand as your hands go up. Blow out as your hands return to your side. Breathe in deeply as your arms raise, blow out as arms lower. Do this twice.

Torso Stretches

Stand erect, stomach tight, buttocks tucked under, shoulders pulled back. Grasp hands behind you and straighten arms. Pull up to count of five, release.

Back Stretch

Stand with your back in an L-shape. Feet are apart, knees soft. Now press the small of your back in, arching your back but keeping the L-shape. This is very controlled with your stomach tight as you can. Then release and round your back, keeping the L-shape. Slowly come up to standing position, keeping the rounded-back shape. Repeat. This is an excellent back-strengthening exercise. Be sure to keep the knees soft, never stiff and straight. Let the movement flow.

Straddle Stretch

Excellent for the inner legs, waist, inner and outer thighs, and buttocks. Sit with legs stretched out, knees soft, never stiff. Sit as high as you can, ribcage lifted, stomach tucked in. Now turn to your right foot and gently reach out over that knee, keeping the stomach tucked in, never jerking, but keeping the movement smooth. Very gently, walk your hands forward in front of your body on the floor, stretching forward to the other side where you stretch over your left leg. Hold the stretches for at least a count of five. Do a minimum of four.

Hamstring Stretch

Sitting upright holding in the stomach, breathe deeply and then slowly reach forward from the hips, not the shoulders. Keep the knees soft and bend them if you need to. Grab the toes and hold for a count of five. Then very slowly, round over the knees, feeling the stretch from the hips to the shoulders and along the back of the legs. When you return to a sitting position, come up very slowly, controlling from the abdomen. Sit up tall, breathe deeply in and blow out, then as you lower your body over your knees, exhale. Breathe in as you come up. Repeat five times.

Increasing your strength and flexibility takes time, patience, and commitment. These stretches are designed to prevent injury and create an awareness of technique in your movements. You may also want to learn about using hand weights or the resistance cords (handy for traveling).

Think of yourself as an active person. When we change our behavior we must change the way we think. Think of yourself as a person who includes being physical as an important part of life. Look at the following:

- If you bowl one game you use 100 calories. Bowling once or twice a week will result in a loss of eighteen pounds in a year.
- Gardening three days a week for an hour each day will result in a loss of twenty pounds a year! Each hour you spend making your garden beautiful uses 228 calories.
- If you don't like to swim, try just walking in waist-deep water. You'll be using 500 calories per hour. Just one hour a week, or four times for fifteen minutes, and you've lost 52 pounds in a year!

	Lying	Sitting	Standing	Walking	Workout	Stretch
THE JOY OF EXERCISE						
Type of Activity						
6:00						
7:00						
8:00						
9:00						
10:00						
11:00						
12:00						
1:00						
2:00						
3:00						
4:00						
5:00						
6:00						
7:00						
8:00						
9:00						
10:00						
11:00						
12:00						
Totals						

KNOW YOUR HEART FOR TOTAL BODY FITNESS

FOR FLEXIBILITY	FOR THE HEART AND TOTAL BODY	TO BUILD STRENGTH
WARM-UP AND COOL-DOWN STRETCHES *(total body workout)* relaxes specific muscle groups used in strength and aerobic workouts; helps reduce muscle soreness, stiffness; 10 minutes	**AEROBIC DANCE** *(total body workout)* moderate to high intensity; low- to high-impact; increased flexibility and coordination; 45 minutes	**CALISTHENICS** *(total body workout; good for muscle endurance)* no equipment required; the more advanced can increase benefits with arm and leg weights; 20 minutes
	BICYCLING *(good for lower body)* moderate to high intensity; low-impact; outdoors, ride 10 to 20 minutes longer to compensate for coasting; 30 minutes	**FREE-WEIGHT TRAINING** *(works the total body)* exercises general muscle groups; dumbbells are portable and inexpensive; 30 minutes
	JOGGING *(for cardiovascular health)* works lower body; high intensity; high-impact; can do it anywhere; 20 minutes	**WEIGHT-MACHINE TRAINING** *(works the total body)* isolates specific muscles and works them to their maximum throughout motion; controlled movements decrease risk of injury; can buy for home use; 30 minutes
	RACE WALKING *(works both upper and lower body—move those arms!)* moderate intensity; medium impact; great way to break into an exercise routine; 45 minutes	
	STAIR CLIMBING *(works lower body and heart)* moderate to high intensity; low-impact; tones and strengthens legs and buttocks; 30 minutes	
	SWIMMING *(great for total body, especially upper)* moderate to high intensity; low-impact; minimal stress on musculoskeletal system; 30 minutes	

SAMPLE WEEKLY EXERCISE LOG

Activity	Monday	Tuesday	Wednesday	Thursday	Friday	Saturday	Sunday
Target Heart Rate _____ Comments:							

Make sure not to take two or more days off in a row, because it can be hard to get started again. If you want a four-day program, try for a schedule such as Monday, Wednesday, Friday, and Saturday. Remember that consistency is the key to success.

12

CREATING AN ACTIVE LIFESTYLE

It's not exactly headline news that overeaters and food abusers don't like to exercise. Jim is a man who weighed nearly 300 pounds when he began *The All-New Free to Be Thin* lifestyle plan. He told us how he once sat in his chair watching the rain leak through the ceiling on the new carpeting for an hour before he got up to do something about it. "I just didn't feel like moving," he explained. He said he could sit in one place, hardly moving, while his agile and thin wife did most of the work in the house.

You don't have to overdo it.

A little at a time and *easy does it* are your rules of thumb. Overweight people are more discouraged than inspired by the demands of physical exercise. Ask the Lord to guide you in how much you should be exercising and what kind of exercises you should be doing.

You may want to take a daily half-hour walk, or bicycle a half hour a day. Perhaps joining a health club would be just the thing for you. The Holy Spirit is your guide and He won't fail you.

A common but wrong belief is that exercise or physical activity will increase the appetite. The truth is that on the whole, we are already overeating for our energy needs. Research studies have proven we eat less as we exercise more. Strenuous exercise before a meal can act as an appetite suppressant. Also, if our regular exercise is enjoyable, it replaces food abuse brought on by boredom and tension.

Most people don't relish the idea of exercising for weight loss because it takes so much work to lose so little. It certainly isn't inspiring to know that you'd have to run up and down the stairs of the Empire State Building for four hours to lose one pound of body fat!

The rule of thumb again is slow and easy. Don't get yourself discouraged. A little at a time is fine! Try something like walking to the store instead of taking the car. Or running in place for 30 seconds a couple of times a day. Easy!

A person could lose nine pounds a year just by climbing the stairs to his or her fourth-floor office and back down four times a day instead of using the elevator.

On the other hand, if you are inactive, you must rigidly control your calorie intake or you *will* gain weight quickly. If you exercise moderately and regularly, you will not only feel better, but you'll be using up more calories.

Be good to yourself! The next time a friend suggests going out for a cup of coffee, convince her to go for a walk with you instead.

Instead of making your nights out centered around a restaurant and eating, do something active like swimming, walking, jogging, playing volleyball, bowling, tennis, golf, basketball, Ping-Pong, or badminton. If you don't know how to do any of these things, learn. You are in charge of your life. You create your own circumstances. How about kayaking, fencing, tap dancing, or ballet? If you've never played tennis and you go for your first lesson feeling terribly self-conscious and unhappy about all the exercise involved, just tell yourself the truth: It may be difficult now, but it won't be as you improve through practice. You're learning about new, fun physical activities. You're trying out new things and having new experiences. How wonderful!

If you live in the city and are discovering that exercise costs money, you can find cheap ways of doing physical activity. Walking and jogging are free. If you decide to jog, do it along a route where lots of other people jog. There you'll see many overweight people jogging for fitness and health and you won't feel so self-conscious. You don't have to be a track star to jog!

Walking is just as beneficial as jogging—it just takes longer to get where you're going. Walking is something you can do for free and it's great fun. Swing your arms, walk briskly, breathe deeply. You'll wonder why you didn't do it sooner.

When driving your car or sitting at your desk, hold your stomach in for a count of 20—and release. Do it again. Do that a few times a day. Another good exercise is to stand on tiptoes and then lower your heels—up and down, up and down—5 or 10 times a few times a day.

You don't have to be an Olympic champion to be strong. You

don't have to be "the athletic type" to enjoy a couple of physical activities that will bless your body. (How many times have you heard an overweight person shrug off exercise by saying, "I'm just not the athletic type"?)

One of the main excuses for avoiding physical exercise is that we think exercise means lifting weights at the gym, strenuous calisthenics, or some other laborious and exhausting activity.

EASY is the word. Take it easy, and enjoy your exercise. Be like the forty-year-old woman who emphasized our deep breathing in her *exercise plan*. She began doing her deep breathing as her only form of exercise. Her "learn to eat, not diet" program had a powerful impact on her. As the weight fell off, she added more exercises. By the time she reached her goal weight (a loss of 30 pounds), she was in better shape than when she was a teenager actively involved in sports. She felt better and healthier than she had in years.

If you start slowly and do exercises you enjoy, you can add more as you become stronger. Don't forget to give yourself rewards. At the end of each week do something special for yourself.

Along with your daily food plan as outlined in detail in *The All-New Free to Be Thin Lifestyle Plan*, keep a record of your exercise. It's a wonderful feeling of accomplishment when you add up several miles of walking, for example.

PRAYER

Father, I want to serve you. I want to obey you. Show me how to begin creating an active lifestyle for this wonderful body you've given me. Amen.

Basic Walking Program

Preferably exercise 5–6 days per week, but not less than 3

Week	Warm-up (walk slowly)	Target Zone (walk briskly)	Cool-down (walk slowly)	Total Time
1	5 min.	5 min.	5 min.	15 min.
2	5	7	5	17
3	5	9	5	19
4	5	11	5	21
5	5	13	5	23
6	5	15	5	25
7	5	18	5	28
8	5	20	5	30
9	5	23	5	33
10	5	26	5	36
11	5	28	5	38
12	5	30	5	40

Reprinted with permission from *Obesity & Health*. Copyright © 1990.
Healthy Living Institute, 402 S. 14th Street, Hettinger, ND 58639.

Your Target Zone

Your target heart rate, or best activity level, is
60 to 75% of your maximum heart rate.
Higher may be too strenuous, lower provides
little conditioning for your heart and lungs.

Age	Target zone (beats/min.)
20	120–150
25	117–146
30	114–142
35	118–138
40	108–135
45	105–131
50	102–127
55	99–123
60	96–120
65	93–116
70	90–113

13

YOUR DAILY POWER TIME

From the outset, we have emphasized spiritual renewal along with a renewed commitment to physical health.

We have covered some important information so far, and we now return to the foundation of *The All-New Free to Be Thin* lifestyle plan: Every morning have a time of Scripture reading and communication with the Lord. This time with Him is important. A good place to begin your Scripture reading is in the book of Colossians. From there you could read the other books of the New Testament, combined with the *Psalms* and *Proverbs*. You must go to the Lord for your supply of strength for the day and for your instructions. This is vital!

Things you will need:

1. A small notebook, your journal
2. Pen or pencil
3. Bible

For maximum benefit, you will probably want to use *The All-New Free to Be Thin* lifestyle plan personal journal as a helpful companion.

JOURNALING

The purpose of the journal. In your journal write the scripture verse you read for the day and what it means to you. Begin each entry with a scripture verse and then apply it to yourself, making it personal. Then on a separate page or section keep a food diary.

Every morning in your Daily Power Time include a time to talk to the Lord about your food plan for the day. Concentrate on what you want to happen that day. What choices will you make? Talk to the Lord about your exercise plan for the day. Write your plan in your journal.

Make your goal to eat only what you have written down for the day. You will be examining fat content, carbohydrate value, energy value, and protein. You will be eating fiber, fresh fruits and vegetables, and whole grains, and avoiding foods with white flour, sugar, and saturated fats.

Thousands on the original *Free to Be Thin* weight-loss plan kept a calorie count sheet every day. On *The All-New Free to Be Thin* lifestyle plan, we aren't concentrating on calories only. We are learning the joy of having *control* over and knowing all that goes into our bodies.

Why a food diary and journal? Here is what Neva tells Overeaters Victorious groups: "Being accountable for our food choices is a form of discipline. Discipline is a sign that you are a loved child of God! The Word says that we should not reject the discipline of the Lord. He disciplines those whom He loves [see Hebrews 12:5–6]. Discover Jesus' love through the discipline of counting grams of carbohydrates, protein, and fat in your diet. Be glad for the discipline you show by every ugly food you don't eat!"

There are some people (not you, of course) who protest the idea of keeping a journal. Here are some excuses they might use:

"Somebody else might read it and discover my secrets."

"I don't have time."

"It's too much bother."

"I don't have the privacy to do it."

Please don't allow these or any other excuses to rob you of the enormous benefits of keeping a journal. Many men and women on *The All-New Free to Be Thin* lifestyle plan carry their journals with them during the day. Women carry them in their purses along with a small-sized Bible. Men can carry them in their brief cases or lunch boxes.

One woman said, "I don't think I really knew myself at all until I began reading my own journal entries. I can't tell you what a revelation it has been. I'm discovering me!"

WEEKLY EVALUATION

At the end of the week review your journal entries and ask the following:

What new principles has the Lord taught me this week?

How can I be more faithful in honoring the Lord next week?

How have I honored the Lord with my exercise this week?

How have I honored the Lord with my eating this week?

What new changes am I seeing in my attitudes toward:
　Food?
　Exercise and being more active?
　Discipline?
　God?
　Myself?

Food abusers dislike the idea of discipline when it comes to eating. They eat to compensate for the lacks and failures in their lives. You are waging a war against your own reasons for over-eating. You are fighting for the real you to emerge. *Don't be afraid of discipline.*

Using the *All-New Free to Be Thin* lifestyle plan will help you:

1. Be sure you don't miss your Daily Power Time of reading the Word and praying early in the day.
2. Record in your journal what the assigned verse is for the day and what it means to you. Enter your thoughts, feelings, and moods, too.
3. Record the food you will eat for the day (see the next page for a sample chart).

Because your commitment to the Lord is becoming strong and overcoming overeating is real and wholehearted, you *will* succeed.

SUMMARY

Keep your journal. Try not to miss a single day. This discipline is good for you! Think of it as an honor to do it unto the Lord.

FOOD DIARY

Date _____   Calories _____

Breakfast		
Fiber		
Carbohydrates*		
Vegetable		
Fruit		
Protein		
Fat		
Dairy†		
Lunch		
Fiber		
Carbohydrates*		
Vegetable		
Fruit		
Protein		
Fat		
Dairy†		
Dinner		
Fiber		
Carbohydrates*		
Vegetable		
Fruit		
Protein		
Fat		
Dairy†		
Snack		
Fiber		
Carbohydrates		
Vegetable		
Fruit		
Protein		
Fat		
Dairy†		

*Complex Carbohydrates: This plentiful category includes all whole grains, cereals, pastas, flours, breads, crackers, legumes, and starchy vegetables. Some grains are: wheat, oats, barley, rice, rye, cornmeal. Also included are the breads, muffins, etc., prepared *without* refined fats or oils. So many choices and combinations! The possibilities are unlimited.

†Dairy products: Be sure to itemize them under the "fat" category as well as protein if they are not skim or fat-free.

Keep a daily record of your food intake at *each meal.* Know how many grams of fat, fiber, and protein you are eating each day. Remember the amount (see chart).

In cooperation with God, you are gaining control over food. Food will no longer control you.

But thanks be to God that, though you used to be slaves to sin, you wholeheartedly obeyed the form of teaching to which you were entrusted. (Romans 6:17)

You're free now—free to learn discipline and the satisfaction and integrity it will bring you!

PRAYER

Thank you, Lord, for teaching me discipline. Thank you, Lord, that I am now free to be in charge of what I put in my body. I choose to receive from you the strength I need to be faithful to my commitment to you. Your strength fills me. You show me that I can be responsible for what I choose to eat.

I thank you, Lord, that I am victorious in you.

I will accept the discipline of my Daily Prayer Time.

I will read the Word in the strength of the Holy Spirit.

I will keep my daily food diary and be aware of the contents of the food I eat.

I will not be a slave to food any longer.

I am victorious because you are victorious!

In Jesus' name. Amen.

After you have prayed this prayer, pray it again.

14

Praise the Lord and Pass the Celery!

You *can* burn up fat without wearing yourself out or starving half to death. Does this sound too good to be true? It's not. You can eat *fat-fighting* foods.

Many vegetables, for instance, are so low in calories that the metabolic process of digesting them takes more calories than is in the vegetable itself. Take celery, for example. It requires approximately 25 calories of energy to digest one cup of cooked celery or two stalks of raw celery. There are only 10 calories in the celery itself, so by eating 2 stalks of celery you've burned up 15 calories!

There are many fruits and vegetables that are fat-fighting foods. Some of them are:

apples	cherries	oranges
green beans	cucumbers	parsnips
beets	eggplant	pomegranate
blueberries	grapefruit	raspberries
broccoli	grapes	radishes
brussels sprouts	lemons	spinach
cabbage	lettuce	tangerines
cantaloupe	mushrooms	strawberries
carrots	nectarines	tomatoes
cauliflower	onions	watermelon

Your body will use more calories digesting fresh fruit, such as oranges, than if you drink only the juice.

Not only do these foods actually help you burn up body fat,

they are rich in vitamins and minerals that form the fat-fighting enzymes.

As we have said, you need to be aware of the fat content in your foods, and know what portions to eat. One woman neglected to check her fat counter for the amount of fat in chicken. She thought it was a low-calorie, high-protein food. She had decided to eat only chicken for three days. (Unwise and unhealthy!) But when she told us that she had gained nearly five pounds eating two chickens a day she was deeply upset. She had no idea how much fat she had been eating! She had been putting over 200 grams of fat in her body when the daily requirement is only 44 grams. She was also mistaken in thinking there were only 100 calories in half a chicken. Actually she was eating 1,200! When she added carbohydrates, vegetables, and fruit to her diet, she was eating enough for two or three people without knowing it.

Don't let a lack of knowledge lead you to discouragement and to taking your eyes off the goal.

Let your eyes look straight ahead, fix your gaze directly before you. (Proverbs 4:25)

Manny, an Overeaters Victorious member from New Jersey, says, "I'm fighting an addiction! I'm a food addict with a dependency on food just like the drug addict or the alcoholic. My only weapon is the Word of God. I take one day at a time. The Lord says in His Word He won't forsake or leave me."

With your goal set before you, you will succeed.

WHEN YOU SHOP FOR FOOD

Clothe yourselves with the Lord Jesus Christ, and do not think about how to gratify the desires of the sinful nature. (Romans 13:14)

Write these words at the top and on the margins of your shopping list in bold letters:

MAKE NO PROVISION TO FAIL

Arm yourself with the scripture verse you studied that day. Speak it to yourself and feel the peace and loving support of the Lord surround you.

Be sure when you go shopping that you go *after* you've eaten. Do *not* go to the grocery store hungry. Determine to pass up the free food samples high in fat and salt. The free samples may add up to more fat than your daily allowance. With God's Word in your heart, your shopping list of nutritious foods in your hand, set your eyes with a fixed purpose, your gaze straight before you. You're not going to stop and browse around at the pastries.

A most helpful tip is: *Stay close to the walls.* Do most of your shopping along the walls where you'll find the produce for your fresh fruits and vegetables, the meat, poultry and fresh fish, the baked items for whole grain foods and the dairy section for your non-fat milk, cheeses and yogurt. Plan exactly what you'll be buying in the middle aisles and never linger or wander.

Be good to yourself. Take time to relish at the delight you'll find in the produce department. Notice how beautiful the fresh fruits and vegetables are arrayed. Enjoy buying your whole grain foods, low-fat dairy products, low-fat fish, meats, and poultry. As your shopping cart fills, you will have a happy supply of healthy, energy-building meals to bring home for the week.

"But my family loves junk food!" you may protest. "They hate anything that even resembles healthy food." Your family enjoys eating only high-calorie, low-food-value junk food, you say.

But so did *you* at one time. You once ate health-destroying foods, too. Your family hasn't changed yet. Letter after letter arrives at the Overeaters Victorious office from women who are discovering they are the major contributors to their family's poor eating habits.

If you have a family addicted to junk foods, slowly wean them onto a healthier diet. *Slow* is the key word. Start by making luscious fruit salads, broiled fish and poultry (skip the rich gravies and substitute natural juices), and fresh steamed vegetables. Try making healthy fruit and vegetable juice drinks in your blender. For snacks, try introducing raw nuts and seeds, fresh fruit, and low-fat yogurt. Instead of the sugar-packed cereals in the morning, try feeding your family a breakfast of whole grain cereal, fresh fruit, and whole grain breads or muffins baked with polyunsaturated vegetable oil, or none at all. Motivate your loved ones with good-tasting nutritional yummies and your good example.

INVENTORY TIME FOR YOUR CUPBOARDS

Is there food in your kitchen that shouldn't be there?

You may have a lot of food stored in the house, so this next step will take some time and effort on your part.

Take inventory of your cupboards, taking out each can, box, and package, and read the labels. The purpose of this inventory is to learn what you are putting into your body and the bodies of your loved ones. Studies have proven most of us do not read labels, nor are we aware of the content of the foods we put into our mouths. Taste has often been the most important thing to us.

But you are losing your old eating habits. You are changing! You are becoming healthier, thinner, and *smarter.*

"Be wise as a serpent," the Bible tells us. Wise means able to reason and think. When you pick up a package of cereal and see that the first item on the ingredient list is sugar, and there's also a list of preservatives and chemical additives plus a heap of calories to each serving, stop and reevaluate whether or not it is wise to eat it.

Diane was one of the first Overeaters Victorious *Free to Be Thin* group members to take inventory of her kitchen. She took all the food from her cupboards and spread it out on the counters. On one side she put the food she could eat and on the other side the food she couldn't eat. Then in another place she piled the food she didn't want anybody to eat.

She did the same with the food in the refrigerator and in her pantry. She used her journal / calorie log notebook to write lists of products that were nutritious as well as low in calories. The members of her family were not on a weight-loss program, so they could eat certain foods she could not. But she didn't want them eating the junk food that had filled her cupboards for so long. It would take some gradual and loving retraining on her part to wean her family off the rich, gooey desserts and the fast foods loaded with excess fat, sodium preservatives, and chemical additives.

"It was a real shock to me to discover what was actually inside those boxes and cans. I learned that I was more influenced by advertising and commercials than I was by the truth. If the commercial on TV said that a food was nutritious and healthy, I went out and bought it. If an advertisement in a magazine had a picture of someone suntanned, healthy, thin, and smiling next to a food product that was really junk, I'd buy it because the advertisement made it look healthy. I didn't realize what I was do-ing."

Diane was like thousands of Americans who listen to the ac-tor on TV dressed in a doctor's coat telling you that a certain product is good for you. She bought the product without reading the label or finding out the real truth.

We talked to Diane 15 years later and she told us how her life has never been the same since losing 30 pounds and becoming a health-conscious person. "My kids are now older and my daughter, who is married, cooks with nutrition in mind first! When I started *Free to Be Thin,* my family called me a health nut. Now we're all health nuts and healthier and stronger for it! I'm glad you've added the workout program because that's what I'm concentrating on now."

READING THE LABELS

A young mother said, "Sugar is addictive. I know that. I have read about refined sugar and I know that it is just like putting poison into our bodies. It is addictive and makes one's appetite scream "More! More! *More!*" It makes my children either hyper or slow and drunk. It makes me retain liquid. It makes me sick and it makes my teeth rot. I have to ask myself, *Do I need to eat so much of it? Is this an area in my life that is out of control? Can I wholly and honestly feed sugar-laden foods to my family?* I want to be victorious and wise. The responsibility is mine."

You may not think you eat much sugar, but when you take inventory of your cupboards and your refrigerator, you'll be sur-prised at what you discover. There's sugar in catsup, pickles, mayonnaise, soups, Jell-O, canned fruits, most cereals, and all salad dressings. Sugar is often labeled as "carbohydrates" and this may confuse you, an unsuspecting buyer. You may also see these words on labels—they mean sugar:

Dextrose is a chemical sugar, derived synthetically from starch. It is also called corn sugar.

Fructose is fruit sugar.

Maltose is malt sugar.

Lactose is milk sugar.

Sucrose is refined sugar (addictive).

Glucose is a sugar found in fruits and vegetables. It is also blood sugar, an essential element in the human bloodstream.

Don't confuse it with the sucrose in soda pop or candy bars. They are not the same. Glucose is important for your health.

The advertisements may tell you that sugar is "100% natural," but so is rattlesnake venom. Read your labels. Know what you're buying!

KNOW YOUR SUGAR			
Food	Amount	Serving	Sugar Equivalent
Candy			
Hershey Bar	1 oz.	1 bar	7 tsp.
Chocolate cream	¼ oz.	(35/lb.)	2 tsp.
Chocolate fudge	½ oz.	1½" sq. (15/lb.)	4 tsp.
Chewing gum		1 stick	⅓ tsp.
Lifesaver		1 regular size	⅓ tsp.
Cake			
Chocolate cake	3½ oz.	2 layer icing (¹⁄₁₂ cake)	15 tsp.
Angel cake	1½ oz.	1 pc. (¹⁄₁₂ large cake)	6 tsp.
Sponge cake	1¾ oz.	¹⁄₁₀ of average cake	6 tsp.
Cream puff (iced)	3 oz.	1 average custarfilled	5 tsp.
Doughnut plain	1½ oz.	3" in diameter	4 tsp.
Cookies			
Macaroons	1 oz.	1 large or 2 small	3 tsp.
Gingersnaps	¼ oz.	1 medium	1 tsp.
Brownies	¾ oz.	2×2×¾"	3 tsp.
Custards			
Custard, baked		½ cup	4 tsp.
Gelatin		½ cup	4 tsp.
Junket		½ cup	3 tsp.
Ice Cream			
Ice cream		½ cup	5 to 6 tsp.
Sherbet		½ cup	6 to 8 tsp.
Pie			
Apple Pie		⅙ of med. pie	12 tsp.
Cherry pie		⅙ of med. pie	14 tsp.
Custard, coconut pie		⅙ of med. pie	10 tsp.
Pumpkin pie		⅙ of med. pie	10 tsp.
Sauce			
Chocolate sauce	1 oz.	1 heap. tsp.	4½ tsp.
Marshmallow	¼ oz.	1 aver. (60/1 lb.)	1½ tsp.

(Continued on next page)

Food	Amount	Serving	Sugar Equivalent
Spreads			
Jam	¾ oz.	1 T level or 1 heap. tsp.	3 tsp.
Jelly	¾ oz.	1 T level or 1 heap. tsp.	2½ tsp.
Marmalade	¾ oz.	1 T level or 1 heap. tsp.	3 tsp.
Honey	¾ oz.	1 T level or 1 heap. tsp.	3 tsp.
Milk Drinks			
Chocolate (whole milk)		1 cup, 5 oz. milk	6 tsp.
Cocoa (whole milk)		1 cup, 5 oz. milk	4 tsp.
Soft Drinks			
Coca-Cola		1 bottle, 6 oz.	4⅓ tsp.
Others		6 oz. glass	4⅓ tsp.
Cooked Fruits			
Peaches, canned in syrup	½ oz.	2 halves, 1 T juice	3½ tsp.
Rhubarb, stewed	3½ oz.	½ cup sweetened	8 tsp.
Apple sauce (no added sweetener)	3½ oz.	½ cup scant	2 tsp.
Prunes, stewed, sweetened	3½ oz.	4 to 5 med., 2 T juice	8 tsp.
Dried Fruits			
Apricots, dried		4 to 6 halves	4 tsp.
Prunes, dried		3 to 4 med.	4 tsp.
Dates, dried		3 to 4 stoned	4½ tsp.
Figs, dried		1½ to 2 small	4 tsp.
Raisins		¼ cup	4 tsp.
Fruits and Fruit Juices			
Fruit cocktail	4¼ oz.	½ cup, scant	5 tsp.
Orange juice	3½ oz.	½ cup, scant	2 tsp.
Grapefruit juice, unsweetened	3½ oz.	½ cup, scant	2⅕ tsp.
Grape juice, commercial	3½ oz.	½ cup, scant	3⅔ tsp.
Pineapple juice, unsweetened	3½ oz.	½ cup, scant	2⅗ tsp.

*Fredericks, Carlton. *Low Blood Sugar and You.* New York: Grosset & Cunlap, 1969.

WATCH THAT SALT

The body needs a certain amount of sodium, but most of us eat far too much. You need only about 250–500 milligrams of dietary sodium a day. That's about one-fifth of a *teaspoon* of salt. You will be eating that much in your natural foods on *The All-New Free to Be Thin* lifestyle plan. We know that excess salt contributes to high blood pressure. Your kidneys are designed to eliminate excess sodium, but when you overwork this system with large amounts of salt, it makes it more difficult for the kidneys to do their work. Excess sodium that is not excreted causes fluid retention. Too much salt can contribute to or aggravate disorders such as angina, congestive heart failure, and even stomach cancer. It can increase calcium excretion and heighten the risk of osteoporosis.

It's an amazing thing to eat food and actually taste it! When your food is loaded with salt, that's what you're tasting—salt! Salt on labels can be read as monosodium glutamate (MSG), baking soda, or sodium nitrate.

One of the best things about cutting down on salt is the fact that your food begins to taste so wonderful. Your taste buds will revel in all the new flavors. Low sodium is easy too. The good news is many foods are now low-sodium or sodium-free. All the food products that make a controlled sodium claim must follow the Food and Drug Administration's standard for labeling:

- "No salt added" means that no *extra* salt has been added, but it may still have been processed with salt or sodium compounds.
- "Reduced sodium" has 75% less sodium than normal.
- "Low sodium" has no more than 144 milligrams of sodium per serving.
- "Very low sodium" means no more than 35 milligrams of sodium per serving.
- "Sodium-free" means the product contains less than 5 milligrams of sodium per serving.

You will also want to read labels for sea salts, kelp, baking soda, baking powder, onion, garlic, and celery salt, sodium saccharin, sodium nitrate, sodium propionate, and anything with the word *sodium* in it. Particular culprits are catsup, chili sauce, worcestershire sauce, and barbecue sauce.

Read your labels!

DON'T PLAN FOR FAILURE

Sue, after taking an inventory of her cupboards, learned that she had a habit of tucking certain fattening, unhealthy items away for future failures. In case there would be a day when she didn't want to stay on her *Free to Be Thin* lifestyle plan, there was something in the cupboard to fail with, something fattening and calorie-loaded.

Don't plan for failure. Plan for success! If you plan to succeed, you will succeed.

Fill your cupboards and refrigerator with foods that are low-fat, low-sodium, and rich in vitamins, minerals, and fiber. If your family eats foods that you have removed from your diet, keep them out of sight. Don't leave cookies in see-through containers if they're tempting to you. Don't leave dishes of candy around on tables if you're tempted to eat it. Don't store the cake where you can see it (especially if it has already been cut). You may be tempted to eat the crumbs and "shave off a thin slice"—and then miserably discover you've shaved off and eaten half the cake. In addition, clear the table when you're finished eating so you don't eat up the leftovers.

Marge gained five pounds one week even though she thought she rigorously stuck to her food plan. She realized that nibbling on the leftovers was the culprit. The crisp end of the roast beef, Junior's frosting from his cake, a lick of the peanut butter on the knife, the cake crumbs from the cake pan, the last of the gravy in the pan, the leftover macaroni—"just a teensy taste."

Those teensy tastes can be devastating. One little ounce of cheese puffs contains 348 milligrams of sodium, 10.0 grams of fat, and 14 milligrams of cholesterol (not to mention 159 calories). One little cup of party mix (cereal, pretzels, nuts) has 722 milligrams of sodium (that's almost your total daily intake), 23 grams of fat, and 312 calories. *Ouch.* One tablespoon of grape jam has 50 calories. Half a cup of potato salad has 662 milligrams of sodium! It also has 11.5 grams of fat and 86 milligrams of cholesterol. One measly honey bun has 33.3 grams of fat and 675 milligrams of sodium! The extra nibbling you do throughout the day may be more dangerous than you think. That is why your food journal is so important. Writing down every bite that goes into your mouth will help you see and understand habits you've been unaware of.

You are committed to changing your eating habits and getting your body under submission to the Holy Spirit. You are making no provision for the flesh and its lusts. You are no longer a person who has no control over what foods go into your body.

By taking an inventory of your cupboards, you will find out some interesting things about yourself, as well as learn more about the foods you buy. You may discover, as one woman shared in her group, that she had been buying candies and sweets "for her children," but she would hide them in the back of the cupboard so she herself could eat them, somewhat the same way as the alcoholic may hide liquor bottles. Those high-sugar, high-fat, high-sodium foods you think you're buying for your family, children, or friends have a way of never getting past you.

Perhaps you're like the woman who buys packaged pastries "for the family." But on the way home from the store in the car, she eats one, then another. She feels guilty about bringing home the pastries with two missing, so she finishes the whole package. That's 115.80 grams of fat, 978 milligrams of sodium, and an incredible 1,356 calories.

Or maybe you've had the same experience as the man who bought half a gallon of ice cream "for the family" and ate every spoonful himself.

Check your motives for buying foods. Make no provision for failure. If having ice cream in the freezer is a stumbling block for you, don't buy it.

Let your eyes look straight ahead, fix your gaze directly before you. (Proverbs 4:25)

Make no provision for *failure.* Your goal is to be healthier, more active, and stronger for the glory of God.

After you have eliminated the junk foods and high-fat foods from your cupboards and supplied your shelves with plenty of healthy, fresh foods and filled your refrigerator with fresh vegetables and fruits, low-fat, low-calorie, low-sodium and nutritious foods, you can stand back and feel terrific. You can see you are really serious about your commitment. Your desire really is to glorify God in your body. It isn't just talk. You are acting on your commitment! You know your changes come from within— they are becoming a *part* of you. You are free to be thin!

The average overweight person goes on 1.5 diets per year and makes over 15 major attempts to lose weight between the ages of 21 and 50. Their attempts almost always fail and the next year they're back on another diet.

Thousands of books on losing weight are sold each year; there's a billion-dollar business in over-the-counter pills, powdered drinks, chewing gums, gadgets, exercise devices, and a host of other items promising a thinner you. You can rejoice that you are doing more than just reading a book. *You are acting on a commitment to the Lord. He is there beside you to help you.*

You have taken inventory of your cupboards. You are changed. You are changing your eating habits. You know how to shop. You have chosen an *active* life.

> *It is for freedom that Christ has set us free. Stand firm, then, and do not let yourselves be burdened again by a yoke of slavery.* (Galatians 5:1)

You're not a slave to food when you're in control of what you eat. Bondage is slavery. And a slave has to do everything his master tells him. The cookies in the cookie jar can beat against the lid and scream your name if they want, but you are now listening to the strengthening, guiding voice of the Lord. The pastry shop and ice cream store can appear so inviting you can almost hear them shout "Come have some!" from across the street. But you're not their slave any longer. You're free. You can say *no.* And at home there is nothing in your cupboards to hold you captive. You won't be prowling out of bed at 3 A.M. to eat some ugly, fattening thing. You're free from that bondage. You're free to be healthy and beautiful to the glory of God. You make no provision for failure.

PRAYER

Dear Lord, thank you that I am free to be in control of what I eat. Show me, Lord, the mistaken thinking that has held me in bondage. Show me, Lord, the deceptions that have caused me to overeat and harm my body. I choose to be free in you. I choose to be free from the bondage to food that has caused me to fail.

I repent in the name of Jesus of the deceitful eating I have done in the past. I repent of deviously buying wrong foods and telling myself they were for someone else. I repent of buying these foods, hiding these foods, and eating those foods.

Thank you, Lord, for the strength and direction you constantly give me. Thank you, Lord, for your great love for me. In Jesus' name. Amen.

15

DECIDING TO LIVE

DANIEL'S CHOICES

Daniel, a man of God in the Old Testament, was not without his problems. Right from the beginning, he needed to make some important choices about his lifestyle and eating habits. He knew how God instructed His people to eat, and he was dedicated to his Jewish traditions. But in the first chapter of Daniel, when Jerusalem was besieged by the Babylonians, Daniel was one of the young men taken captive to serve in the court of the foreign king, Nebuchadnezzar.

This king wanted Israeli boys who were

1. Good-looking
2. Intelligent in every branch of wisdom
3. Endowed with understanding and discerning knowledge
4. Possessed with an ability to serve in the king's court

When these young men were taken to the court of the king, they were to be instructed in the literature and language of the Chaldeans for three years. They were to eat the king's choice food and drink the wine he drank. Then, at the end of their three-year education, these "chosen" ones were to enter the king's personal service.

Have you ever considered yourself in training for the King of Kings' personal service? Do you believe yourself to be among those "chosen" for God's service?

In the New Testament, the apostle Peter writes to "chosen ones" who are aliens in foreign places. These aliens "who have been chosen according to the foreknowledge of God the Father, through the sanctifying work of the Spirit" (1 Peter 1:2).

A Christian is an alien *without* going to a foreign land. We're aliens because in an ungodly world we are born-again spiritual people. This is our earthly dwelling place until the day we show up on the doorstep of our real homeland, heaven.

One woman, upon studying this verse, told her group, "I'm an alien in my own body! I don't belong in such a self-destructive pattern of eating. The real me wants to live in disciplined obedience."

What visible evidence of the fruit of self-control!

There's a little word in this scripture passage that overeaters don't like. It's *obedience.*

The Christian is a chosen alien—chosen "for obedience to Jesus Christ and sprinkling by his blood: Grace and peace be [ours] in abundance" (1 Peter 1:2).

We have been chosen so that we may obey Jesus Christ! Notice that it says, "Grace and peace be yours in abundance." You may wonder why that phrase comes after the word "obedience."

When you are in obedience you have grace and peace in *abundance*! It's a dazzling thought.

That's the place where Daniel was. He saw all those rich, choice foods and wines of the king's and he simply said, "No." (How easy it is to form the word *no* with our lips and how difficult to say it when there are rich, fattening foods around!)

Daniel and his three friends were the only ones who refused the king's food and wine. Daniel made up his mind *that he would not defile himself* with the king's choice food or with the wine he drank (Daniel 1:8).

Have you ever thought that your overeating was *defiling*?

Defile means to make filthy or dirty; befoul. It means to tarnish the luster of; render impure, corrupt. Further definitions are to make unclean or unfit for ceremonial use; desecrate and to violate the chastity of.

Think of the last time you binged on ugly, fat-ladened food. Ask yourself:

How did I feel after eating food that hurt my body?

Were the feelings I had worth it?

When we overeat, and avoid exercise, it's not our bodies or our health we're thinking of. We're more intent on satisfying an emotional need. When you sit down to dinner, do you think about your heart, lungs, colon, blood pressure, or tissue and muscle needs? Probably not. You're thinking about how hungry you are and how good the food looks and smells. You couldn't care less about your vital organs or metabolism.

After my painful surgery where I [Neva] had the intestinal bypass reversed, my physician told me I could expect some weight gain. I was horrified. Depressed and upset, I left the doctor's office and went directly to a restaurant where I ordered a piece of pie, complete with a dollop of whipped cream. After eating it, I sat there feeling worse than ever. I heard within my heart the Spirit of the Lord speak to me: "*Now* do you feel better?"

It's important to look at your feelings *while* you overeat.

Smokers have similar unconcern for their bodies' needs. A male patient, aged 42, is in a hospital with cancer of the throat. It's painful and life-consuming. In spite of his body screaming for an end to smoking, he continues to puff on cigarettes every day. His doctor is adamant. "If you don't stop smoking, you'll die!" he pleads. The man looks him straight in the eye and says, "Then, I'll die."

> *Those who live according to the sinful nature have their minds set on what that nature desires; but those who live in accordance with the Spirit have their minds set on what the Spirit desires.* (Romans 8:5)

BEING CONSCIOUS OF WHAT YOU EAT

Decide now to stay conscious of what you're eating at the time and the effect it has on your body. Don't be one of those who finds himself or herself holding an empty box and wondering who ate all the cookies. Pay attention to what you eat.

Most food abusers have no idea what the food they are eating is doing to their body. They also aren't aware of how full they are. The foods we are suggesting on *The All-New Free to Be Thin* lifestyle plan are so delicious that you will become more alert and aware of what you are eating and how much. It is exciting to be healthy and it is exciting to eat healthy. It's when you are eating junk foods, sweets, and foods loaded with sodium that you slip into a vacuous mind-set. It's almost as if someone else is feeding you and you don't have anything to do with it.

GETTING A GRIP

Selfishness is something you can control. Uncontrolled, our sensual, natural desires are wild and unruly; they kick their heels, rear their heads against anything in the way. We become selfish, unthinking, propelled by stupid, meaningless passions. Your flesh has nothing good about it *unless* it is under the dominating influence and power of the Holy Spirit.

When your sinful nature is in control, you'll defile your body at every chance. If you're at a party and there are rich foods on the table, you'll gobble them up without a thought. You may even continue to eat when you get home. Then you may find yourself on a full-fledged gorging binge!

The sinful nature is miserable and wretched; it doesn't know how to make a single wise decision. It always acts against the will and beauty of God.

It is beautiful to listen to the Spirit and obey the Word of God. Romans 8:6 says, "The mind of sinful man is death, but *the mind controlled by the Spirit is life and peace.*"

One woman shared how she read a book on dieting in one sitting and by the time she finished the last chapter, she had eaten six chocolate bars and polished off a quart of orange soda. (One 12-ounce can of regular soft drink has nine teaspoons of sugar! One chocolate bar has seven teaspoons of sugar.)

She said, "I should have had diet soda," but the unhealthy chemicals and additives and excess sodium in artificially sweetened sodas make up for the missing calories. Diet sodas are not a good choice. Their high carbonation contributes to flatulence and bloated stomach. Water is a much better beverage. Choose water instead. Drink eight glasses of water every day.

If our bodies had voices, the first things they might say to us would be, "Stop putting that junk into me!" and "Exercise me!" They do speak to us, in fact—not with words, but with pain, disease, lack of strength and vitality, nervous disorders, headaches, and sleeplessness.

One woman tells how she was killing herself with her eating habits and lack of exercise. "And all the time I was nagging my husband about his smoking and watching TV. We were both killing ourselves—he with nicotine and I with a fork and spoon and sedentary habits."

Daniel was chosen to serve a king, Nebuchadnezzar. You and I are chosen to serve the King of Kings. Our old ways may have hurt our bodies with our undisciplined appetites, but now we choose *not* to defile our bodies. We choose *not* to eat the destructive foods that do not feed us, but in fact destroy us.

"Those controlled by the sinful nature cannot please God"

(Romans 8:8). The incongruous thing about some Christians is that in church they'll worship God in spirit and truth and have a wonderful spiritual time. Then after church they'll run home and wolf down all sorts of unhealthy foods. It seems odd to be in the Spirit one minute and then as soon as food is brought into the picture, we abandon our spiritual mind and jump right into self-destruction.

> *The sinful mind is hostile to God. It does not submit to God's law, nor can it do so.* (Romans 8:7)

Daniel did not abandon his spiritual mind. He refused to defile himself and resisted the temptation of the king's food. He chose a high-fiber, healthy diet of no added sugars and fats. He convinced the commander of the officials to allow him and his friends to eat their own diet for ten days. He told the overseer to see for himself at the end of the ten days if they were not healthier and more robust than all the youths who had been eating the king's choice food.

Naturally, they were healthier and more robust than all the others. So the overseer agreed to continue withholding the king's choice foods and wine so they could *stay* on their healthy, high-fiber, whole-food diet. Notice the word *stay*. Daniel wanted to *stay* with God's plan.

He wasn't doing penance by eating a vegetarian high-fiber, low-fat diet and drinking water. Far from it! He wasn't on a crazy crash diet or short-term slim-up program. He *wanted* to eat healthy foods. He didn't consider the king's choice food to be desirable at all. He found those foods distasteful and repugnant.[1]

What do you think of when you say the word *delicious*? If you think of some rich, salty thing, *stop*. You can change your ways of thinking. No longer consider the king's choice food as delicious. Think of those foods as ugly, undesirable.

Food is not meant to tantalize and torment us. Food is meant to bless us and strengthen us. It is meant to satisfy our bodily

---

[1]Daniel's diet was a total lifestyle and was beautifully balanced—rich in vitamins, minerals, and protein. It would have included combinations of such vegetables as cabbage, onions, celery, cucumbers, lettuce, greens, tomatoes, potatoes, peas, lentils, and various beans. If you decide to eat like Daniel, be sure to eat vegetables, fruits, grains and milk products that include all the necessary vitamins, minerals, and protein your body requires. Remember, you need at least 44 to 56 grams of protein a day. Be sure to know what vegetables to eat for proper balance. Otherwise, you're going on another fad diet.

needs for nourishment. Stuffing ourselves with unhealthy dainties will never satisfy the tiniest spot of our appetite. Our unruly, unhappy appetite always calls out hungrily, "More! More!"

You can train your mind to stop thinking of unhealthy food as delicious, tantalizing, luscious, mouth-watering, or any other such adjectives. Set your mind to change. After committing yourself to Jesus instead of overeating, you must train your mind to think about winning the battle with food. What *is* delicious?

On *The All-New Free to Be Thin* lifestyle plan you will find your tastes changing. The men and women who were successful on the initial *Free to Be Thin* program marvel at the change in their taste. "I was amazed at myself!" says Dani, a successful businesswoman in California. "I was a confirmed junk-food junkie. I was the type who would salt the salted peanuts."

Dani, who changed her eating habits and lost 30 pounds, sings the praises of her new lifestyle. She made the change gradually, beginning by adding to her diet fiber in the form of fresh fruits and vegetables.

"The first time I ate a baked potato sprinkled with pepper, fresh basil and chives, without the butter and sour cream, I was amazed—I *liked* it!"

Slowly, Dani eliminated fast-food lunches and take-out, high-sodium dinners. She began bringing her lunch to work. She also learned how to order in restaurants.

"I order broiled fish and meat, lots of yummy veggies, baked potatoes, wheat breads, fruit—I'm telling you, food never tasted so good."

Dani has lost interest in rich pastries and heavy, greasy, salted foods. Refined, processed foods no longer attract her. She radiates when she says, "The Lord has truly made me free and *kept* me free! I exercise every day and feel the best I've ever felt in my life."

YOU ARE WINNING!

When an athlete goes into a game, he or she is psyched up to win. The coach talks *Win*, the cheerleaders sing and cheer *Win*, the crowds in the stands shout and wave banners, *Win*!

What do you tell yourself when you're out on the field fighting to overcome overeating? *Win, Win, Win*? Or do you tell yourself pitiful words like, "Oh, poor me. Everybody else gets chocolate pie. I get carrots"?

There's tremendous power in your mind—God has given it to you. You have a strong will. You can choose to use it. Daniel made up his mind and did exactly as he purposed to do. Blame Satan all you want, but he doesn't eat the food—you do. Satan may tempt you, but you're still the one who does the eating.

It's your mind Satan appeals to. That is why it is vitally important that you reclaim your mind from his influence and put it where it belongs—under the power and influence of the Holy Spirit who loves you.

King Nebuchadnezzar talked with the young men, and out of all the youths he had recruited, none were found like Daniel and his friends. When Daniel ate according to the wisdom of the Holy Spirit, he was rewarded not only with good looks and a healthy body, but also God's blessings of

1. Knowledge and intelligence in every branch of literature and wisdom
2. Understanding of all kinds of visions and dreams

He and his three friends were ushered into the king's royal service and, once in, they proved valuable to King Nebuchadnezzar. When the king consulted them regarding matters of wisdom and understanding, he found them ten times better than all the magicians and conjurers who were in his entire realm.

Their high-fiber vegetarian diet was not the only reason for these young Jews' tremendous godly power, of course. Clearly, they prospered because they loved and obeyed God. The food was just the means God used to draw them into the intimacy with Him as only He can do.

FIBER IS ONE OF YOUR BEST BLESSINGS

On *The All-New Free to Be Thin* lifestyle plan, you'll be eating lots of wonderful fiber, or "roughage." Soluble fiber helps to lower your cholesterol. Oat bran, beans, and carrots contain soluble fiber. Insoluble fiber found in wheat bran and grains helps your elimination. Fiber helps to move chemical impurities out of the system. It is imperative to include fiber in your diet.

If you have colitis, diverticulitis, or some other stomach and intestinal disease, check with your doctor before adding more fiber to your diet.

If you have been eating mostly white breads (even though the package says "enriched"), processed canned foods (canned beans and franks have 16 grams of fat, 15 milligrams of cholesterol, and 1105 milligrams of sodium in *one* cup!) as well as frozen foods and fast foods like pizza and burgers, you've been literally starving yourself. In addition to your damaging intake of fats and sodium, you're not getting enough fiber.

Don't think your grilled chicken and bacon burger is a "health food" because it's served on a whole wheat bun. It contains 39 grams of fat (that's your total daily allowance if you're a woman), 60 milligrams of cholesterol, 610 calories (not including the french fries and beverage), and *973 milligrams of sodium*!

Some high-fiber foods are listed on the chart on page 123. Familiarize yourself with these.

HEALTHY ELIMINATION

If you are new to *The All-New Free to Be Thin* lifestyle plan, you should begin to have healthier elimination within ten days. You may possibly experience some stomach gas with the added fiber in the diet, but don't let it concern you. It won't last. A *Free to Be Thin* group leader humorously tells her group, "If you're worried about beans giving you gas, just eat them with a friend."

When you change from a diet of refined food to a healthy eating lifestyle of high-fiber meals of delicious fresh vegetables, fruits, and whole grains, it's possible to experience some flatulence. It will be temporary and it's perfectly normal.

Some suggestions to eliminate abdominal bloating and gas not due to pathological conditions are listed below. These are good general guidelines to follow for improved digestion and absorption of your food, as well as for healthy elimination.

1. Do not eat quickly.
2. Avoid stress when eating. Try to eat in a relaxed manner.
3. Chew your food thoroughly before swallowing.
4. Avoid fatty or fried foods.
5. Avoid sweets, except fruits.
6. Steam or microwave your vegetables.
7. Avoid swallowing air as you chew or drink.
8. Drink a minimum of eight glasses of water daily.
9. When you have the urge to go, go! Do not retain a bowel movement.
10. Exercise daily and regularly.

FIBER CONTENT OF SELECTED FOODS

Food	Serving	Insoluble Fiber (grams)	Soluble Fiber (grams)	Calories
GRAINS				
Bread, whole wheat	1 slice	1.2	.3	61
Barley, pearled, dry	2 Tbsp.	1.0	1.5	97
Cornmeal, whole grain	2 Tbsp.	1.8	.2	54
Oat bran, dry	⅓ cup	2.2	2.0	90
Oats, regular, dry	⅓ cup	1.5	1.3	100
FRUITS				
Apple, with skin	1	2.1	.9	80
Banana	½ medium	.7	.3	46
Dates, dried	2	1.2	.4	50
Figs, dried	1 medium	2.9	3.7	55
Strawberries	1¼ cup	2.0	1.2	60
Orange	1 small	.9	.3	40
VEGETABLES				
Broccoli, cooked	½ cup	1.1	.9	28
Brussels sprouts, cooked	½ cup	2.3	1.6	30
Cabbage, Chinese, cooked	½ cup	1.2	1.6	30
Cauliflower, cooked	½ cup	1.1	.5	14
Corn, cooked	½ cup	2.7	.2	71
Kale, cooked	½ cup	1.4	1.4	20
Peas, young green, cooked	½ cup	3.0	1.1	57
Onion, cooked	½ cup	1.4	.8	32
Potato, white, baked	½ medium	1.0	.9	73
Yam, cooked	½ medium	1.4	1.5	80
BEANS				
Kidney beans, cooked	½ cup	3.3	2.5	115
Lima beans, cooked	½ cup	3.2	1.2	64
Pinto beans, cooked	½ cup	3.3	2.0	114
Lentils, cooked	½ cup	1.1	.9	58
Peas, black-eyed, cooked	½ cup	6.8	4.5	145

Source: James W. Anderson, *Plant Fiber in Foods* (Lexington, Kentucky: HCF Diabetes Research Foundation, 1986); James W. Anderson, "Dietary Fiber Content of Selected Foods," *American Journal of Clinical Nutrition* 47 (1988):440–447; and the Quaker Oats Analytical Laboratory as printed in *The New Pritikin Program* (Simon & Schuster, 1990).

Daily Requirement of Fiber	
For Women:	**For Men:**
20–40 grams	39–60 grams

For maximum benefit, eat foods as close to their natural state as possible. Our favorites are broccoli, brussels sprouts, cabbage (if you have a problem with gas in the beginning, steam or cook these instead of eating them raw), potatoes, and corn. And the fruits are limitless: apples, pears, oranges, berries—what an array!

Legumes give you double the benefit because they are not only high in fiber, they are excellent protein sources. Beans such as garbanzos, also called chick peas, are wonderful. Whip these up in the blender with low-fat plain yogurt, garlic, and oregano and you have a delicious hummus dip for your whole wheat pita bread!

Red kidney beans, black-eyed beans, lentils, or black beans are great to have along with rice and a big vegetable salad. Try a savory black bean burrito on a corn tortilla with cilantro, salsa, and shredded romaine lettuce. *Olé!*

Chronic constipation is sometimes caused by too much animal protein in the diet and resultant putrefaction in the intestines. Other causes are dehydration (not drinking enough water), liver disfunction, over-refined foods, and vitamin and mineral deficiencies, particularly vitamin B, inositol, and potassium.

The All-New Free to Be Thin lifestyle plan emphasizes *high-fiber* food for optimum health and vitality. High-fiber foods require more chewing than refined and animal foods. They are energy foods and less likely than fats to be stored as extra pounds; they are necessary for healthy elimination. On *The All-New Free to Be Thin* lifestyle plan, you get all the fiber you need.

A NEW HOPE

Praise be to the God and Father of our Lord Jesus Christ! In his great mercy he has given us new birth into a living hope.
(1 Peter 1:3)

Five years after the publication of *Free to Be Thin,* Neva and I wrote another book called *There's More to Being Thin Than Being Thin* in response to the overwhelming success of the Overeaters Victorious *Free to Be Thin* program. In that book we talk about leaving the past behind and where we go from here. We were once slaves to our old, former nature, which was prone to selfishness and failure. Now, by working hand-in-hand with God toward a happier and more fulfilled life, we can become all we were meant to be.

At one time we may not have been aware of the promises of God, but now, according to 1 Peter 1:4, we have an inheritance that can never perish, spoil, or fade—it is kept for us. We, through faith, are shielded by God's power.

Can you see the dramatic contrast between your old self and your new self? Now you can enter God's beautiful plan for your ultimate best. Your body will consistently feel better and you will no longer be deceived by rationalizing or denying, or by lazy and undisciplined habits. You will no longer lie to yourself.

Now, please say these words out loud:

I obey the Lord.
I choose to obey the Lord.
I am a person of obedience.
Following the Lord is not penance.
Change is not punishment.
Health is a blessing.
Lack of exercise robs energy.
I will obey the Lord.
I will not defile my body.
Absentminded eating defiles.

If you eat a chocolate eclair on the way home from the grocery store, it's not the eclair that disobeys. It's you.

Look at rich, unhealthy foods not as fattening but as defiling. The members of an Overeaters Victorious *Free to Be Thin* group discussed what defiled food meant to them. One woman said she could never eat something if she found a hair in it. No matter how hungry she was, if there had been a hair in it, she wouldn't touch it. Two of the men felt the same way about flies or cockroaches. If they were ever to find a fly or cockroach in the food, it was to them defiled. Another woman said if food fell on the floor, she wouldn't eat it. (However, most food abusers have said they don't have a problem with food that has fallen on the floor, and indeed, some have even said they've removed food from the garbage, brushed it off, and eaten it.)

A woman in New York baked a layer cake in her oven. When the cake had finished baking, she opened the oven door and found a dead, cooked rat stretched across and stuck in the cake. Unknown to her, there had been a rat in the oven when she put the cake in to bake. Would you say that cake was defiled?

You wouldn't want to eat a hair, a roach, or a rat, but are you in or out of control when you reach for that eclair or those greasy french fries? They may be just as defiling. Do you have your hand in the garbage? If you are disobeying God and eating more than you should, cry out to the Lord for help to keep focused. He won't turn His back on you. He is right there to help you.

If you are eating too much salt, fat, or sugar, don't ever give up! No matter how many times you stumble, get up and go on. God loves you and doesn't give up on you. As long as you are alive, there is hope.

Remember this promise:

He who began a good work in you will carry it on to completion until the day of Christ Jesus. (Philippians 1:6)

He's not going to forsake you in your hour of need. And if you stumble, He's not going to throw His hands in the air and give up on you. God granted Daniel favor and compassion (see Daniel 1:9) when he chose to obey. He will grant you favor and compassion, too, when you choose to obey, because He loves you just as much as He loved Daniel.

PRAYER

Thank you, Father, for favor and compassion in my eating habits. I have committed my eating to you, Lord, and I am committed to you. I will obey you, Lord, and eat as you show me. Give me wisdom and knowledge so that I can make healthy choices.

I choose not to defile myself, as Daniel chose not to defile himself. I need your help and strength, Lord. In the past I have made poor choices regarding food and I have been a food abuser. I have been inactive and unfaithful in my exercise program. Now, because my mind is set on the Spirit, I have life and peace and a new strength. I choose obedience. I choose you. In Jesus' name. Amen.

16

DELIGHTED AND FULFILLED

Eddy woke up with a sugar hangover. He had a headache, felt lethargic, and was ill-tempered. He was accustomed to eating a diet rich with sugary foods, but lately he had consumed more than usual. His diet almost entirely consisted of sweets and sugar drinks.

Sugar is a culprit. We remember the days when we thought of Jell-O as a diet dessert. Jell-O is 83 percent sugar! Are you aware of other supposedly nonfat food items such as

Coffee-Mate—65% sugar
Cremora—57% sugar
Cool Whip—21% sugar
Hamburger Helper—23% sugar
Shake 'N Bake—51% sugar
Wishbone Russian Dressing—30% sugar
Quaker 100% Natural Cereal—24% sugar
Ritz Crackers—12% sugar
Skippy Creamy Peanut Butter—9% sugar

Ironically, Eddy always used no-cal sweeteners in his coffee. He knew he had to change. His health was deteriorating, his body was bloated and weak, and his psychological state was in shambles.

Delight yourself in the Lord and he will give you the desires of your heart. (Psalm 37:4)

Once Eddy began his *Free to Be Thin* lifestyle plan, he realized it was not going to be just for a few weeks or months. He realized it was *forever.* Daniel in the Bible didn't eat vegetables and water for ten days only and then binge on the king's food the eleventh day.

You are going to be eating the Lord's way, restoring your body's health. You'll never want to go back to the old ways. You remember all too well those diets and programs you've tried. You remember the bondage and the pain of weight cycling and feelings of defeat.

Eddy needed to discover joy in his new eating habits. He decided not to defile his body with the wrong foods any longer. He began to write in his journal daily.

Eddy was a single man when he came to an Overeaters Victorious *Free to Be Thin* group. He took careful inventory of the cupboards in his kitchen and he removed the junk food that had gathered. He concentrated on *feeling* good, and he exercised.

He said he was so shocked when he learned apple pie ala mode (his favorite) had huge quantities of sugar in it plus fatty shortening that he never touched it again. One year later Eddy had taken off 67 pounds and was running in his first 5K race. That was five years ago and today Eddy, now a married man with one child, lives a life of health and energy. He has not had a sugar or salt hangover in 5 years.

If it is a trial for you to eat differently than your friends, remember Psalm 37:4. When you watch the commercials on TV for rich and fattening foods, turn your head away. In the old days just the sight of fattening, sugary food may have aroused a response in you. No more!

A subtle pitfall for the food abusers is to be around the foods they have removed from their eating plan. Some people, while they are changing their eating habits, will spend more time in the kitchen than they need to. They will touch, feel, handle, and prepare foods with intense interest. Their delight in food is still there, even though they are changing their habits. One woman prepared a picnic dinner for her family, consisting of a whipped cream Jell-O salad, potato salad, and hot dogs stuffed with cheese, and although she did not eat any of it herself, she had gained a certain pleasure handling and preparing foods that were essentially unhealthy.

Even though she didn't eat one morsel, a week later when she was feeling discouraged and something had upset her in her personal life, do you know what she did? She made a huge bowl of potato salad and sliced wieners and ate the entire thing herself. She became so ill her husband was afraid she was going to die.

It's important that we don't take an inordinate delight in food. Especially in foods that will hurt our bodies. Do you still describe rich, sugary foods as "scrumptious" or "delicious" or "out of this world"? They aren't! One particular disgusting food product, loaded with sugar and chemicals, is described as "heavenly." What an insult! Heavenly food is healthy and vitalizing, not loaded with sugar, white flour, preservatives, chemicals, salt, and fat.

DELIGHT YOURSELF IN THE LORD

He is our delight. Food is not our delight.

Can you imagine Daniel sitting in his room, complaining miserably that he couldn't eat the king's greasy casserole? Can you just see Daniel sneaking out of bed at night and heading for the king's kitchen in search of a jelly doughnut or bowl of chocolate ice cream?

No, it was Daniel's idea to refuse the king's food. Daniel purposed in his heart he would not defile or hurt himself. Affirm these powerful truths:

I Will Not Hurt Myself By . . .

- Talking about, thinking about, looking at, or handling ugly, fatty, sugary, or salty foods
- Lying to myself and telling myself that unhealthy junk food won't hurt me
- Not exercising
- Not keeping my journal
- Missing my Daily Power Time with the Lord
- Giving myself sugar hangovers

Your new desire is to love the Lord, to serve Him with your body, soul, and mind.

Delight yourself in the Lord and he will give you the desires of your heart (Psalm 37:4).

THE DESIRES OF YOUR HEART

Are you asking God to take away an ungodly appetite? If you are, be sure you are not delighting in ungodly *thoughts* about food.

Be aware that you can lust for ungodly foods even though you're not eating them. Jesus warned us of the dangers of lust (Matthew 5:28). It can capture and control you. If you believe the junk foods you used to hurt your body with are "delicious" or appealing, you're radically mistaken.

When you ask God to take away your ungodly appetite, He will help you as you replace it with knowledge about your own body and intelligence in the matters of food and nutrition. He frees you! If you're abstaining from ugly, fattening foods but are still drooling over them, *stop immediately* and change your way of thinking. Your delight is in *the Lord* and in thinking *His* thoughts!

Remember, your tastes are changing. I can truthfully tell you that I have not found anything appealing in the ugly foods I used to have a problem resisting. My taste has completely changed. It's one of the most wonderful benefits to *The All-New Free To Be Thin* lifestyle plan.

Communication with God includes the attitude of your heart as well as your words in prayer. You communicate with God by the attention (or lack of attention) you give Him. Delight yourself in the Lord, and your whole being will adore Him. Your whole being is then fulfilled.

"Delight yourself in the Lord and he will give you the desires of your heart." Who gives us our desires when we are submitted to God? God himself. It was He who gave you the desire to be free. Your desire is *His* desire and your delight is in Him.

Eddy had his *desire* in the right place—that is, he desired to *obey* the Lord. He *desired* to change his eating habits and eat unto the Lord. Eventually he delighted in his choices.

Delight means a "high degree of pleasure or enjoyment; joy; rapture; great pleasure and satisfaction; to please highly."

Eddy wanted to know how to delight in the Lord with his eating. He meditated on Psalm 37:4 and told his group that he was learning to read labels and examine the contents of the food he ate, but it wasn't always easy.

"Do everything without complaining or arguing" (Philippians 2:14) was the Bible verse he wrote in his journal. "When I was young, my father was very strict with me. He was always saying no to this or that. I couldn't do the things the other kids did or go places with them. I always obeyed him, but I resented his rules. I felt deprived.

"Now I see that I was the same way with the Lord. I would

do what I knew was right, but I didn't like it. Not eating the junk food I had been eating was like being deprived again and I blamed the Lord."

Eddy learned that he was deceived. He learned to delight himself in the Lord and obey Him. It is Satan who deprives us and deceives us by suggesting that ugly foods are delicious. He influences us to eat ungodly foods and not exercise. Junk food is not delicious or wonderful.

God is a giver. He *gives,* restores, lifts up, builds, strengthens, and blesses. It is Satan who destroys, kills, murders, lies, and deceives. God is all truth and love. Satan has no truth or love in him and he relishes to see you sick and unhealthy.

Do you know what your own true desires are? The verse we are looking at in Psalms reads, "He will give you the desires of your heart." Is it your desire to be strong and healthy? If it is, then ask yourself another question: Am I doing all I can to co-operate with God so that He can fulfill my heart's desire?

DESIRE-ACTION WORKSHEET

If it is your desire to be healthy, you will want to cooperate with the Lord so that you don't get in the way of His fulfilling your desire. On *The All-New Free to Be Thin* lifestyle plan, it is a good idea to keep a Desire-Action Sheet such as the one we show here. On one side write your desire. This desire to be healthy is one that He gave you in the first place. So write His desire as well as your own when you write *your* goals. On the other side you write what God is having you do or change in your life so He can bless and fulfill your desire.

Delight in your new eating program. Delight in your commitment to the Lord. Delight in your minimum daily requirements. Delight in self-control and obedience to the Lord!

In the thousands of letters we have received from successful Free to Be Thinners, the most common remark is that losing weight has been a secondary benefit. The first benefit is the spiritual development and growth that has taken place. Most of the weight programs today concentrate on weight loss only, falling short of healing the whole person; spirit, soul, and body. The goal of *The All-New Free to Be Thin* lifestyle plan is to live wholly free.

Jean said that although she had lost 60 pounds on the *Free to*

DESIRE	ACTION
1. I desire to have more energy. 2. I desire to be stronger and healthier. 3. I desire to be free from the tyranny of overeating. 4. I desire to be more in control of what I eat at coffee breaks.	• I will follow *The All-New Free to Be Thin* lifestyle plan by knowing the contents of food. • I will watch the fat content of the foods I eat. • I will not exceed my sodium daily requirement. • I will eat the required amount of fiber. • I will keep my journal. • I will exercise every day. • I will plan and make "portable" healthy snacks to take to work.

Be Thin program, her real joy was in learning to hear from the Lord. She learned, much to her joy, that the Lord delights in speaking to us personally and directly. She learned to hear His voice and gentle urging, not audibly but in the quietness of her heart.

"I really *delight* in the Lord," she told a group of new Free to Be Thinners. "Through becoming strong and healthy and learning to think of myself the way the Lord thinks of me, I am a new person. What the Lord did in my heart and life is wonderful! I am new through and through."

Delight yourself in keeping your journal and your daily food plan sheet. It is not a drudgery or a hindrance! It is your freedom and your blessing. Thank God for discipline! Thank God you can be healthy! Thank God He is fulfilling the desires of your heart because your desires are His desires. That's how close you are to Him. You are special and dear to Him. Your eating habits are spiritually guided now.

Make a Desire-Action Sheet for each week. What can I do this *week*? Keep it in your journal and refer to it as the week progresses. The reason for this is that you could write on the desire side, "To lose 10 pounds," and then a year later, you're still 10 pounds overweight. Your desires *work together* with your actions to produce results. Write your weekly exercise desire. Example: "Lord, this week it is my desire to exercise by walking every day." Then decide how and when to do it. Set a time and be regular to exercise at that time every day.

Also, on the "Action" side of the paper you might write, "Be faithful every day." Well, you can't be faithful without the Lord.

You need your Daily Power Time with Him to strengthen your faith. You may want to add some more Bible reading time to your day.

One woman wrote as a desire, "To spend more time with the Lord." As an action she had to decide just how she was going to do that, and she had to be specific.

The Lord wants us to be specific. Being indecisive and vague never brings beautiful, eternal results.

For example: In order to spend more time with the Lord, I will turn off the TV set. I will get up half an hour earlier in the morning to pray and read the Word. I'll walk and listen to Scripture and teaching tapes on my Walkman. I'll allow myself time every night before going to bed to pray and read the Word.

What would *your* specific actions be?

SAYING ONE THING—DOING ANOTHER

One good result the Desire-Action Sheet has is revealing the inconsistencies in our words. Often we talk about obeying but we blatantly disobey. We'll pray, "Oh, Lord, I just want to be your obedient servant. I want to delight in you with my heart and soul," and then we'll run to the refrigerator for some sugary so-called "treat."

The Lord doesn't reward us with ugly, unhealthy "treats." He rewards us with power and strength in the Holy Spirit.

Double-bind type communication is saying one thing and meaning another. I push you away, but I'm saying, "Please love me." On one side of my Desire-Action Sheet I say, "I want to obey you, Lord," and then I skip breakfast and lunch. By three o'clock I'm so hungry I stop at the Dairy Queen and wolf down a double hamburger with cheese (980 milligrams of sodium, 37 grams of fat, 650 calories) and a peanut butter parfait (figure it out—that's 250 milligrams of sodium, 34 grams of fat, and 740 calories!). Need we say more?

You may discover you are a lot more self-willed than you ever dreamed. But thank God, Jesus is a Savior. *He saves us from ourselves!*

We are learning to say one thing and, at last, do the same.

PRAYER

Dear Savior, I have given you the right to be Lord of my body. I need to know how very close you are to me. It is amazing and wonderful to me that you will give me the desires of my heart. I am beginning to understand the meaning of the word *delight*. Thank you, Lord.

17

The Deadly Anger Trap

Sandy insisted she was large-framed and that's why she was overweight. Her roommates assented and offered no protest. The truth was, Sandy had 238 pounds on her mesomorph (medium-sized) frame. At 5'4", she was plainly an overweight overeater. She ate from the moment she woke up until she went to sleep at night.

"For he [the Lord] knows how we are formed," reads Psalm 103:14. Sandy blamed her overweight on heredity, metabolism, and a number of other excuses, but she didn't acknowledge *overeating*. Sandy's body type was not one that would allow her to be a healthy, vigorous Size–1 Petite, but she *could* be free from the overeating habits that would eventually destroy her health. She could discover the root causes of her overeating behavior and finally be delivered from their hold on her life.

Richard Weed, an actor and college instructor from Minneapolis, now teaching in Spain, was doing grade reports one day when a student approached him and asked to see his grade on an exam.

"What? You mean I only got a *C* on that exam?" the student exclaimed in surprise.

"Yes. That's what you earned," Richard responded. "What would you rather have gotten as a grade? An *A*? Or a *B*?"

"Well, I don't know—"

Richard handed the student his pen. "Why don't you put the grade you feel you deserve in the grade book. Here, go ahead. Do you want an *A*?"

The young man was speechless.

Then the wise teacher said, "I'll do it for you. I'll erase the *C* and write an *A* in its place."

When he finished he looked long at the surprised student.

"Tell me," he said, "do you know the material any better now?"

We are what we are, no matter what lies we may tell ourselves. We may want to give ourselves *A's* when we have earned *C's*. And conversely, we may downgrade ourselves. (That's equally deceitful.)

Lack of honesty can be a symptom of rebellion and anger. If you can be dishonest in a small thing, you can eventually be dishonest in something big. That "something big" might be your covenant with the Lord. You promise to eat a high-fiber lunch, but you rebel and eat an unhealthy white-bread sandwich stuffed with high-sodium so-called lunch meat. Or you promise the Lord that you will live for Him and His ways, and then haughtily deny your commitment and do something cruel to another person. The Lord wants to save you from the deceitfulness that can tempt you, and instead give you a beautiful, wholesome, and complete life in Him.

Read Isaiah 30:1:

> *"Woe to the obstinate children," declares the Lord, "to those who carry out plans that are not mine, forming an alliance, but not by my Spirit, heaping sin upon sin."*

Are you ever obstinate? Look at the following checklist. Do any of these statements fit you?

- ☐ I eat without thinking about what I'm eating or how it may defile my body. After I've eaten I feel repentant and remorseful.
- ☐ I don't have anything else going for me in my life except eating. I don't want to give that up, too!
- ☐ I want my _____ (fill in blank) when I want it.
- ☐ God knows the pressure and problems I've got in my life and that I eat because of them. Why doesn't God remove them if He wants me to be in control?
- ☐ I asked God to take away my appetite and He didn't do it. He must not care.
- ☐ If my husband (or wife) didn't like to eat a lot of fattening foods, I wouldn't have a problem with food.
- ☐ If my wife (or husband) didn't cook such fattening foods, I wouldn't have a problem with food.
- ☐ If my mother didn't cook such fattening foods, I wouldn't have a problem. I come from a family of overeaters and that's why I'm an overeater.

☐ Reading labels is a big chore. If it says "low-fat" or "low-cholesterol," I just figure it must be good to eat.

Add your own statements to the list. You see how dishonest rebellion is? The truth is, nobody else is the cause of your eating problems. Other people and factors may be the stimuli that trigger your overeating. But the person responsible for your actions is *you*.

God wants to take the painful and debilitating anger from us. He wants to free us from that bondage that is worse than any prison. *Whom God sets free is truly free!* God waits for you to be willing to give up obstinate thoughts and actions.

Yet the Lord longs to be gracious to you; he rises to show you compassion. For the Lord is a God of justice. Blessed are all who wait for him! (Isaiah 30:18)

DON'T WAIT UNTIL CONDITIONS ARE RIGHT

Several years ago we received a letter from a man who had been in prison for 14 years and was more than 80 pounds overweight. Neva sent a copy of the letter to all Overeaters Victorious group leaders. The man had read in the newspaper about the *Free to Be Thin* program, and successfully lost 84 pounds while in prison.

Have you ever complained that you couldn't change your eating habits because the "conditions weren't right"? Did you ever tell the Lord you couldn't possibly make good choices when there was a wedding, a luncheon, a party, or Christmas just around the corner?

This man gave his heart to Jesus while in prison. Eating prison food, unable to choose his own menus, he went from 249 pounds to 165. He decided to make some changes in his life and made up his mind to discipline his eating habits and to exercise his body. He chose to change even though conditions were far from "just right."

If you don't think you can possibly make good choices in your present situation, you are mistaken. You *can* do it. God will show you how if you let Him. Take time to listen to Him speak to you. He speaks to you through His Word and in that still, small voice within you.

> *Although the Lord gives you the bread of adversity and the*
> *water of affliction, your teachers will be hidden no more;*
> *with your own eyes you will see them. Whether you turn to*
> *the right or to the left, your ears will hear a voice behind you,*
> *saying, "This is the way; walk in it."* (Isaiah 30:20–21)

You can change your obstinate ways. It is for your good. At the time the man in prison was released on parole, he wrote that he had learned to let God into every area of his life—and to completely change him. "I was so filled with hate and anger, I could easily have killed someone. Going to prison kept me from murder. Now the Lord Jesus has cleansed me and given me a whole new life and heart!"

There are two things that will help us as the Lord works to remove our obstinacy. First:

Be willing to admit your anger. Recognize it.

If you don't believe there's a shred of anger in you, then you won't allow the Lord to work as He tries to remove it. You will get angry with Him, with yourself, and with anyone else around for getting in the way of *your* wants and demands.

Some people do not want to admit they are overeaters and food abusers. An overeater says defensively, "I like to eat! God knows I like to eat. He made me this way, after all. If He wanted me thin, He should have made me a person without an appetite." In effect, this person is blaming God. And if we can blame God for our own atrocious eating habits, we can blame Him for any number of other things in life. He could be blamed for our getting sick, for our car running out of gas on the highway, for a son's lost mittens, for a husband's lack of enthusiasm, for a daughter's broken marriage, for the death of a parent, a rude neighbor's remark, the rain. . . . *We could blame God for everything that ever went wrong in our lives.*

It is not only foolish to blame God for our calamities and sorrows, it is anti-gospel. Many of the events in our lives we call tragedies are not tragedies at all. Difficulties and trials are used by God to show us His love as He helps us overcome these challenges. But we want our own way. Fortunately, God wants His way. He wants to win over our selfish ways in order to make us winners. He wants us to grow strong, full of courage and wisdom.

He understands how we hate to let go of our stubbornness. That's why the Holy Spirit inspired these words in Proverbs

3:11–12, which are repeated in the New Testament in Hebrews 12:5–6:

Do not despise the Lord's discipline and do not resent His rebuke, because the Lord disciplines those he loves as a father the son he delights in.

We delight Him, therefore He corrects us!

If your own father didn't delight in you, you now have a heavenly Father who does. It's a wonderful truth to think about, and if you will meditate on it seriously, you will find it much easier to give up rebellious attitudes.

Do not lose heart when he rebukes you, because the Lord disciplines those he loves, and he punishes everyone he accepts as a son [or daughter]. (Hebrews 12:5–6)

God disciplines us for our own benefit. He chastens *"for our profit, that we might be partakers of his holiness."*

It might not be fun at first because you may really *want* to eat something fat-and-sugar-laden. You may really feel you *deserve* another helping of some rich calorie-coated food. You may be *compelled* to devour something that will only add pounds to you. You may be *driven* to the refrigerator or the cupboards.

The Lord understands these compulsions, drives, and neurotic substitutions for *true* comfort and love. But He wants them conquered.

He wants the rebellion removed. He can do a perfect work *if* you will begin by admitting the rebellion in your heart and life.

The second thing we need to do to help the Lord remove rebellion in our lives is to *allow Him* to do it!

Allow Him the right to remove the rebellion.

Lisa was not in the habit of drinking water. Even though she suffered from constipation, heartburn, and spasms of her colon, she insisted she drank enough liquid during the day and didn't need water. She drank at least eight cups of coffee every day and a couple of diet sodas, as well. In her rebellious attitude Lisa was hurting her body, not to mention the negative psychological effects she suffered.

Lisa was like many others and made the mistake of equating all fluids with water. Water, however, is pure and contains no calories, whereas other drinks are not pure and do contain calories. The sugar included in so many sodas, fruit juices, and processed drinks actually require additional water to digest the drink itself. Coffee and most soft drinks and teas contain caffeine. Caffeine can increase blood pressure and, according to some studies, increase the amount of fatty acids in the bloodstream.

THE JOY OF WATER

Lisa's body craved water, but her rebelliousness drove her to substitute unhealthy choices.

> **You need six to eight glasses of beautiful water a day— every day.**

Water helps the body to use stored fat more efficiently as fuel. The kidneys need a sufficient supply of water to function properly. When you don't drink enough water during the day, the liver is forced to help do some of the kidneys' work. A principal function of the liver is to metabolize fat into usable energy, but if the liver is overworked doing the kidneys' job, its own ability to metabolize fat is impaired. As a result, the body burns less fat as fuel and more fat is stored.

One way to make sure you are drinking enough water is to fill a half gallon container or plastic quart bottle with purified water in the morning. Take that bottle with you or keep it handy and sip from it during the day. I (Marie) carry a bottle of water with me, and in the classes at the university many students sit at their desks with a bottle of water at their side. I have been to public gatherings where nearly everyone has brought their own water. As I'm driving in my car I sometimes look out the window and see other drivers sipping from their water bottles. You can buy the kind that has a straw with it (although if you have problems with intestinal gas, don't drink from a straw). I (Marie) buy a 32-ounce plastic bottle of water at the supermarket, and when I have drunk that I simply refill it with my own purified water from the reverse osmosis system in my house.

WHEN YOU DON'T THINK YOU CAN MAKE IT

No discipline seems pleasant at the time, but painful. (Hebrews 12:11)

"You can say that again!" you declare. "You should see how my friends eat! I'm feeling bad enough as it is and then, on top of it, I have to sit and watch them eat the foods I can't have. What's more, I'm the only one who carries a bottle of water around with me."

Later on, however, [discipline] produces a harvest of righteousness and peace for those who have been trained by it. (Hebrews 12:11)

"But sometimes it's so hard! I get nervous, upset, or just plain tired—and I want to eat! I just can't help myself! Sometimes I just don't think I can make it!"

Therefore, strengthen your feeble arms and weak knees. Make level paths for your feet, so that the lame may not be disabled, but rather healed. (Hebrews 12:12–13)

Your attitudes can be healed. You *will* make it!

Most of us are not aware of how rebellious we have been for most of our lives. How many times have we heard the tearful cry of those on *The All-New Free to Be Thin* lifestyle plan, "I've been angry at life! I've been angry at God, and I've been angry at myself. I have so little self-worth! And I haven't even known it."

Many people write to the Overeaters Victorious office and tell how they had always believed they were good Christians. But there was one corner of their life they stubbornly kept from God, and that was their attitude about physical health—their eating and exercise habits.

One woman said, "I've been on a lot of diets—and each of them out of pride. I'm beginning to realize how many things I've done out of pride. It's hard to admit, but I believe it was pride that destroyed my marriage. I drove my husband away and now he'll never return."

Many painful and even tragic events take place in our lives because of rebellion.

Pride is a form of rebellion because pride resists God's authority and control of your life. Pride is having an inordinate opinion of your own importance, superiority, or merit. God wants to free you—He wants you to be an overcomer.

THE OVERCOMER

Have you ever wondered what it means to be an overcomer? An overcomer:

- Looks at difficulties as opportunities to grow and learn
- Is not a quitter
- Is a perseverer
- Is confident
- Is patient with herself or himself as well as others, and is not judgmental
- Understands God's mercy and grace
- Learns from the past and moves on
- Doesn't insist on always being right
- Dares to make mistakes and gives others the right to make mistakes, too
- Recognizes setbacks are as much a part of the process of overcoming as victory
- Sees that overcoming is not a group activity—it's a personal journey with God
- Knows that overcoming is not a badge you wear—it's an experience one goes through
- Is not alone

An overcomer is not a victim. If he or she behaves like a victim, it does not have to be a life pattern.

Don't say it can't be done. Yes, it can! God will make it happen. He will do it His way, and one way to help Him is to rejoice in what He is doing in your life.

REJOICE EVERMORE

Start attacking rebellion by rejoicing in what God is doing for you. Rejoice in what God is teaching you. Praise the Lord for the food you eat. Thank Him for your new eating program. Thank Him for the new life ahead of you as an overcomer.

There is much for you to rejoice in! He is removing rebellion from you. You will rejoice doubly as you experience the rebellion leaving you.

PRAYER

Almighty God, I refuse and renounce the hold that rebellion has had over me. I admit to rebellion and anger in my life. But I willingly turn from these ways and give you, Lord, the right to change me.

Even though I have been a food abuser for _____ (fill in blank) years, I can be free! Your Word tells me that I do not need to continue as a victim by hurting my body anymore! I am a new person in Christ!

I will not make excuses any longer. I will not demand my own way. I will not hurt my body and mind with self-indulgence, thinking I'm "pampering" myself.

I will not blame others for what I've done to myself.

I will dare to exercise and feel good.

I will be a content and happy person. I will rejoice that you, Lord, are my teacher and you are showing me the way to live. In Jesus' name. Amen.

You see? Genuine self-worth is gained when I realize my own obstinacy and then choose to repent as well as forgive myself and go on.

With godly wisdom and insight, I see my own rebellion and sinfulness and I hate it. And so can you. But then we need to see ourselves as God sees us—and accept the true self-respect and dignity He gives us.

I am an overcomer.

18

BODY BUDDIES

Tanya and Sally were introduced to the *Free to Be Thin* program in 1983. At that time Sally was 100 pounds overweight and her overeating was causing her health to deteriorate. Tanya's food abuse had added 60 pounds to her small (ectomorph-mesomorph) frame, and she was suffering with a string of health problems including joint pain, heart palpitations, and edema.

Tanya and Sally became partners in *The All-New Free to Be Thin* plan and close friends. They were "body buddies" in that they understood and cared for the struggle each had with food and body abuse. Their friendship has flourished to this day, over ten years later.

"In the beginning it wasn't always roses," Tanya explained when sharing about her success and new healthy body. "I was bent on destroying myself. Sally helped me see and understand I was important and valuable—too valuable to self-destruct."

A body buddy is someone who is willing to commit to your new lifestyle program with you. This person will help you reach a point of health and vitality in your life. "Having a weight-loss partner is one thing, but having a friend who is willing to stand with you as you fight against sickness is another," says Sally. "My eating disorder was sick—my body was sick. Tanya wouldn't let me stay sick. That's a real friend."

Both Tanya and Sally have become healthier, thinner, and stronger. They have maintained healthy body weights and have made their *Free to Be Thin* lifestyle plan a part of their lives that they will never want to change.

Two women, Sheila and Karen, who have heavy and demanding work schedules, are also body buddies on the *Free to Be Thin* lifestyle plan. They work out together four to six times a week at their local health club, and remember the days when they hated it. "We used to try to come up with excuses for *not* exercising," says Sheila, "but then Karen would remind me of our promise to God, so we would go—and we'd be so proud of ourselves afterward! It was great."

Sheila and Karen are becoming stronger and healthier. "Being a body buddy is a commitment, and it's really helped me expand and grow as a person. I've always been a loner. I had so much pain and hurt inside that I was denying and ignoring. I had to become responsible."

A body buddy is a person like you who has wisely chosen to change his or her life pattern. Your body buddy will have the same goals and desires as you and will support your good choices and decisions.

Food and body abuse is like an addiction. It's a powerful force that captures the victim in its vise-like grip. From its dark prison the victim catches an occasional glimpse outward at freedom, and then is seemingly overwhelmed with helplessness once again. You are the one who has the ability to change this cruel and painful cycle! And like the abuser of alcohol and drugs, you—the food and body abuser—need support. Your *Free to Be Thin* is one powerful and valuable source of support (see Appendix for information on *Free to Be Thin* groups). Your body buddy will be your friend and encouragement. It can be your marriage partner, one who is committed to a healthier lifestyle, as you are. Neva and her husband, Lee, are body buddies. Lee is committed to Neva's lifestyle plan, understanding her struggles with weight. Neva is dedicated to Lee's lifestyle plan as he battles high cholesterol and diabetes. Choose your body buddy carefully.

Be patient, bearing with one another in love. (Ephesians 4:2)

We've included here the same scriptural guidelines that have been successfully followed by thousands of people on the Overeaters Victorious *Free to Be Thin* program. They are your body buddy guidelines. Read them when you make your agreement with your body buddy and go over them together prayerfully:

SCRIPTURE VERSES TO SHARE WITH YOUR BODY BUDDY

Ecclesiastes 4:8–12—The importance of two partners

Acts 20:35—Help the weak

Romans 12:9–10, 16—Be consistent in your love

Romans 14:21—Don't do anything that will cause your partner to fall

Romans 15:1—Bear with each other's failings

1 Corinthians 8:9–13—Be careful not to be a stumbling block

Galatians 5:14—Love others as yourself

Galatians 6:10—Do only good to each other

Philippians 1:3–7—Pray for each other, be confident that God is at work

Philippians 2:1–4—Be like-minded and look after the interests of each other

Colossians 3:12—Be patient, gentle, and compassionate

Colossians 3:13—Bear with each other

Colossians 3:16—Worship together

1 Thessalonians 5:11—Build up and encourage each other

1 Thessalonians 5:15—Be kind to each other

James 2:14–18—Faith brings action

You Are My Body Buddy

You are my friend, and I love you. I realize that you have allowed me to enter a very private part of your life and our relationship is special. I want you to know that with God's help, I will be faithful to you and to our friendship as we overcome food and body abuse.

When you are down, I will help you get on your feet again. If I too have fallen and cannot pull you up, I will get under you and push. I will provide warmth from the living Word of God when I sense you are growing cold. I will help you when you are weak.

I promise to be consistent in my love for you. And if you want to binge or hurt your body by neglect, don't ask me to be a part of it. I promise that I will not be a partner to your failure, only to your success. I will not cook, prepare, buy, or tempt you in any way with food that is not on your program or in your best interest. I will encourage your physical exercise and be part of it if possible.

If you should lose your way, I will be there to help you and to lead you to the forgiving Savior.

I will not be a stumbling block to you. I love you as I love myself and want only your success. I will give others a good report of the work and victory I see ahead for you.

I promise to pray for you. I am confident of the work He is doing in you. I believe in you. I will keep a special place in my heart for you at all times.

I will keep you in mind when I am tempted to give up, realizing that my success is important to you. When I am tempted to be lax or when I engage in a behavior that will hurt me, I will try to remember that I am a worthwhile, loved person and God wants my very best.

We will be sharing discoveries about ourselves and the root causes of our food and body abuse. I will honor the trust between us.

I will seek creative ways to build you up in faith and encourage you. I always want to seek the good in and for you.

When you need me to be firm, I will be firm. But I will always endeavor to be compassionate, patient, and gentle in my concern for you and ask the same from you.

I choose to accompany my faith in your success with action. In other words, don't expect any fattening goodies from me! Don't expect me to feed your self-pity (should there be any) or to feel sorry for you when you pass up some gooey treat that neither of us needs. And I will not let you make excuses for not exercising.

We will make it this time, my friend! You, me, and Jesus.

Free to Be Thin Lifestyle Body Buddy	Free to Be Thin Lifestyle Body Buddy

19

WHY ARE WE ATTRACTED TO THE WRONG FOODS?

Ever notice how you seem to be magnetically drawn to some foods, and others don't attract you at all? When God first brought *Free to Be Thin* into my life (Marie speaking), I was a person who could not resist ice cream. I simply loved it. I could eat mountains of ice cream at one sitting. I could eat it three times a day. I could have *lived* on ice cream. Now I would no more eat ice cream than a bag of sand. I'm simply not attracted to ice cream. I'm not interested. I've lost my taste for it.

Years ago in the beginning of my *Free to Be Thin* lifestyle efforts, resisting ice cream or frozen yogurt was a chore. Now I don't give it a second thought. But why was I attracted to ice cream in the first place? Often an irresistible attraction to dairy products like ice cream, flavored yogurt, milk shakes, malted milks, and puddings indicate a psychological hunger. I have worked through both the physical and psychological sides of the addiction.

When we admit we are recovering food abusers and food addicts, we realize that overeating is spiritually and psychologically linked. Our cravings have psychological significance. Our eating behavior gives us messages we have been ignoring, and our commitment to *The All-New Free to Be Thin* lifestyle plan will not let us ignore them any longer.

Katie, age 43, had never been more than twenty pounds overweight in her life and most people would not call her fat, but she would go up and down, gaining and losing the same twenty pounds. Her fitness program had been on a yo-yo course, too. Some years she'd be fit as an athlete and then the next year lazy as a hen on an egg. One of the things that helped Katie the most was examining her hunger to be nurtured, comforted, and accepted. Her biggest craving was ice cream, too.

"Dairy products were like *Mom* to me," she says. "Without knowing it, I was a little girl again eating ice cream, and Mom was telling me what a good little girl I was."

Katie had to learn to be her *own* mother and tell herself loving, nurturing words. She needed to hear that she accepted *herself.* Katie's body buddy was of particular help because she continually affirmed her in her efforts to develop a sense of self-worth and self-acceptance.

Have you ever noticed that when you overeat, you don't do it with something like carrots or watercress? When is the last time you *craved* a celery stick? Did you ever binge on lettuce? Your fleshly indulgences are usually something *fattening*—most likely something sweet, like dessert. Sugar and animal fat are addictive. The more you eat, the more you eat again.

Whenever Barbara had a problem as a teenager, her mother would sit down at the kitchen table with her, bring out the chocolate cake or the blueberry pie, and they'd talk over Barbara's problem while eating these and other high-calorie, non-spiritual comforters.

Bev remembers when she was sad or upset as a young girl, her mother offered sweets to help her "feel a little better." If she came home from school upset or crying, her mother sliced her a chunk of dessert or pulled out the fried chicken, and said, "You'll feel better after you eat this."

REWARDS, REWARDS

It is always amazing to us how natural it is for the food and body abuser to deny themselves the best things of life. Carl, a man now in his sixties, has been unhealthy and overweight most of his life. He has lived a life of stress and overwork. Driven to graduate college with honors, to land a good job with a top company, to be the best and buy the best and succeed at all he did, he now faces his later years wondering where the time went and why he didn't take better care of his body.

"I rarely felt really good," he tells us now. "And I didn't even know it. I thought feeling achy and mean-tempered was just my character. I thought my body was naturally pudgy and soft and my chronic sicknesses were due to a weak constitution. I figured my real merit was the fact I had brains. But if I was so smart, why didn't I choose a healthier lifestyle?"

Carl had learned early in his life that achievement brought certain rewards. As a child he was rewarded for bringing home good grades. People gave him approval when he did a job well and excelled. He felt better than others, special. It was rewarding for him to be the *best*.

Carl kept this same behavior in his adult life. But the rewards simply were not the same. The harder he worked, the fewer rewards he got and so the harder he worked. He had no idea of the *true* rewards he craved, but his body was giving him messages all the time.

Carl had to learn *how* to reward himself. He taught himself the rewards of feeling better, of being in better physical shape. His wife, Denise, his body buddy, surprised him with a bicycle for his sixty-third birthday and they've joined a cycling club. They swim three mornings a week and have changed their eating to *The All-New Free to Be Thin* lifestyle plan. The Lord has blessed and helped them. He tells others now he feels better and younger in his sixties than he did in his twenties and thirties.

Forget the former things; do not dwell on the past. See, I am doing a new thing! (Isaiah 43:18–19)

Ask yourself now:

- How do I reward myself?
- Do I reward myself often enough?
- Do I expect others to reward me or do I take responsibility for my own rewards?
- Do I give myself the right to be rewarded?
- Do I settle for less in my life? Why?
- Are the rewards I seek ones that I learned as a child and that no longer work for me?

Free to Be Thinners share how, as children, they cleaned their plates in order to "earn" dessert. Dessert, for them, became far more important than the meal. Later, when they really wanted to treat themselves, they chose dessert. And they may still be tempted to choose dessert.

Are you a chubby member of past Clean Plate Clubs who gobbled up all the food on your plate, even though you were already stuffed to the chin? You did it for the sake of the glimmering, luscious, tantalizing dessert. You gulped down mother's cooking even if you didn't like it—for the glorious reward of *dessert.*

Was that you wiping up every lick of gravy on your plate, choking on those last forkfuls of fried liver because over there just beyond your reach was—too glorious for words!—*dessert?*

Nothing was too dear a price to pay for strawberry shortcake or chocolate chiffon pie, or a similar mess. Did you, at the age of ten, completely wipe out the hunger problem of India by eating every morsel of food on your own plate? You deserved a reward for that, Mom said. Your reward was dessert.

Then later, was that you in line at the school cafeteria, passing right by the beautiful vegetables, salads, and entrees, heading directly for the desserts?

And how about recently? Was that you, when you were feeling a little blue, comforting yourself with a rich and calorie-loaded *dessert?*

The unconscious desire is to reward suffering. Desserts can become that reward.

Desserts can come in many forms. From pastries to finger sandwiches; from dried fruit to homemade fudge. As long as it's something you like.

If you are normally healthy (not diabetic or hypoglycemic) and you crave sweets, it may not be sweets you crave at all. Maybe it's energy you need. Sugar raises the blood sugar level in the body and some people get an energy boost after eating it. It's temporary, of course, and after the boost drops, you feel worse than before. So you eat more sugar.

Psychologically, you may be craving *reward.* Remember the magic word *reward?* Are you working hard and need a reward? Are you putting others' needs before your own? Have you just completed a project or are you doing something difficult? Are you in a particularly stressful time?

All of the above require a reward. How will you reward yourself? Reward doesn't always mean something big or dramatic. And it certainly doesn't have to be something to *eat.* How about the reward of doing something *good* for yourself and your body? During your initial days on *The All-New Free to Be Thin* lifestyle plan, you will want to concentrate and make special effort to reward yourself and your body. Here is a suggestion: How about taking a fitness break?

A FITNESS BREAK

- 15 minutes doing your stretches
- A 15-minute brisk walk preceded and followed by stretching
- 10 minutes of deep breathing and relaxing with an "air bath" for your lungs

Ruthie, a nurse from San Diego, calls deep breathing "air baths" for your lungs. Here's how you give your lungs a healthy "air bath." If possible, do your "air bath" outside in the fresh air.

1. Sitting or standing straight with your head erect and shoulders relaxed, expel the air from your lungs by breathing out.
2. Breathe in slowly and deeply to the count of 10, breathing with your diaphragm and filling your lungs with air without hunching up your shoulders.
3. Slowly release the air to the count of 10.

Repeat at least five times. If you feel dizzy, it is because of the oxygen reaching your brain. It's good for you.

Not only is breathing a reward, don't forget the joy of water. Don't forget the joy of talking to a good friend. Don't forget the delight in reading God's Word and being with God's people.

Another wonderful reward is a fitness weekend. Go camping, skiing, hiking, or bicycling with friends, alone, or with family. Take a canoe trip on a river, go for long walks in the country or go to a health club in the city. Go to the water and swim every day. You don't have to make your fitness weekend an expensive one. You can even do it right at home.

TIRED ALL THE TIME

"But I'm too tired for a fitness break," you may argue. "And a fitness *weekend*? I'd be exhausted before Friday night was over." Some people walk around droopy, tired, and exhausted all the time. If you ask them, "What's new?" they sigh and shrug their shoulders and tell you how tired they are. Worn out. Done in. Beat.

There are times we get tired because our bodies are made of flesh and bones, and we demand too much of it by working too hard or not getting enough rest. It's okay to be tired *some* of the time. A football player may be tired after practice; a flight attendant may be tired after a long run across time zones; a teacher may be tired after days in the crowded, demanding classroom. These examples are not due to anxiety-tiredness.

Here are some other things that make you feel tired:

Allowing yourself to be worried. (Worry is the opposite of trust.)

Allowing yourself to feel nervous. (Ask yourself, "Is this nervousness reasonable?")

Allowing yourself to live in fear. (Restricting, painful, and destructive.)

Allowing yourself to feel anxious. (Be anxious for *nothing*. Don't confuse anxiety neurosis with care and concern.)

WHAT DO YOU DO WITH YOUR ENERGY?

The Holy Spirit doesn't drive you, push you, force you, or overwork you. He doesn't give you so much work that you can hardly finish it without falling to pieces. Let go of your drives and let Him work through you, accomplishing what *He* desires.

If you're craving an energy boost, your true source of power and strength is waiting for you. The Word of God "rejoices the heart." Absorb and apply the truths and power in the Word to your life. Allow its energy to permeate your being, and see how unappealing a piece of candy or a sweet will seem to you.

When you are not in the Word, you're not receiving your power pack of strength and vitality. Your spirit and soul are not fed on the true source of energy. Caffeine or sugar may be what you think you crave, but actually you need *more than these*! You need the power of God!

"A happy heart makes the face cheerful," reads Proverbs 15:13. At the same time, a bad mood makes you tired.

Have you ever noticed how tiring it is to be angry or to dwell on negative thoughts? This is because you were not created to live in negativity. You were created to meditate on the Word of God and communicate with God himself.

As it says in Joshua 1:8, make your prayer: "[I will] not let this Book of the Law depart from [my] mouth; [I will] meditate on it day and night, so that [I] may be careful to do everything written in it. Then [I] will be prosperous and successful."

God does not promise to remove stress and negativity from your life. He promises to give you healthy, sound methods of *handling* them!

One well-known preacher who lost 50 pounds on the *Free to Be Thin* program used to be able to eat two whole pies in one sitting! He was so out of shape he could hardly bend over to tie his shoes. He said he wouldn't have dreamed of stuffing himself with asparagus or cauliflower. That would be *punishment.*

What does reward and punishment mean to you? When you were a child, what were your favorite rewards? Were they "treats" of candy, cookies, ice cream? Were they salty fried snacks like chips, crackers and peanut butter, or french fries? Do you feed the same junk to your own children? When you give your child a treat, is it really a treat?

PUNISHMENT

What does punishment mean to you? Doesn't it mean being deprived of something? When you eat greasy, salty, or sugary foods, you could be depriving yourself of a beautiful body and healthy mind.

The definition of *punishment* is "a penalty inflicted for an offense or fault." You may think you are rewarding yourself by eating wrong foods, but you are really punishing yourself. You may joke about healthy, low-calorie foods as "punishment," but you have it confused. There's nothing at all punishing about proper eating. When you look at some gooey, greasy former reward-type dessert say to yourself, "I deserve better!"

The Word of God gives you wisdom regarding the way you should eat. The Word of God makes you smart, not dumb. You are no longer vain in your imaginings. Your heart is not foolish, nor is it darkened. You're on the road to wisdom and beauty. You no longer profess yourself to be wise while actively showing yourself to be a fool (Romans 1:21–22). You know the difference between punishment and reward.

In your journal, make a list of good things you'd like to give yourself. Maybe it's a long, leisurely bubble bath, a long-distance telephone call to a friend, curling up in your favorite chair and reading a great book. Maybe it's buying something new or going somewhere special. Maybe it's taking time off from a heavy schedule to do nothing at all, or work on a favorite hobby or church project. Maybe it's a long walk in the woods; a slow bike ride around a lake. On your list, write *no foods.* Best of all, to take a fitness break! Don't forget your "air bath"!

Repeat and memorize the following four statments:

1. Food is not a friend.
2. Food does not love you.
3. Happiness and self-esteem go together.
4. You use food, it doesn't use you.

Food is not a friend.	Be aware that the advertisements for food are for one purpose and one purpose only—to get your money. Food is not your friend. It's not your enemy either. It just *is.* If you eat wherever you go and whenever you sit down, you've got the wrong companion. Jesus is the true and faithful friend who loves you with the heart of eternity. He gives you *people* as friends; not food which usually keeps you lonely.
Food does not love you.	Love and food have nothing to do with each other. Even if our celebrations and festive events are always accompanied by food and feasting, the food itself is not love. It is the *people* who represent the love. You might think food represents family, security, love, and acceptance, but you need to find these apart from food. You deserve *real* love and security.
Happiness and self-esteem go together.	Your self-esteem is enhanced by being proud of your behaviors. You will be happier as you feel good about genuine inner changes you're making.
You use food, it doesn't use you.	You say to a pastry, "I don't want to put you into my body even though you used to taste good going down. You aren't of any use to this body. I don't want you." But you say to a ripe, juicy apple, "You would be useful to this body. You will also taste delicious. I want you." Food is fuel!

A woman just beginning *The All-New Free to Be Thin* lifestyle plan returned from a church supper glowing with delight.

The other members of her group were eager to hear how she handled herself at the affair. (They all knew the kinds of unhealthy food usually served at the church suppers.)

"You should have seen all the inedibles they spread out on the tables," she said. "When I think of all the times I've eaten the foods that have hurt my body, I can hardly believe it."

Her friends nodded in understanding.

"Everything was either laced with fat or mayonnaise. Salads mixed with whipped cream, vegetables soaked in creamy cheese sauces, breads spread with butter, sugary, oily date bread lathered with cream cheese, fried chicken, salted chips and nuts, cakes and bars. As I passed along the length of the table, I knew that dish after dish held nothing I could eat. I was really hungry, too. I could have eaten a few of those fruit dishes with the whipped cream and marshmallows and rationalized it by telling myself I had no choice—I had to eat something."

If this hasn't happened to you yet, it will sometime in the future. You will find yourself in circumstances that make it inconvenient to remain on your new eating program. This woman handled it beautifully.

"I just said to all that food, 'I don't want you. I won't eat you. You are unhealthy and do not have what my body needs to feel good. You will not make me stronger. I want to put food into this body that will make it run better.' "

The others understood why she was glowing.

"So I had the most beautiful plate of raw vegetables without dressing. And I ate a bran muffin with it." (Total food values: fat, 5.1 grams; fiber, 2 grams; cholesterol, 16 milligrams; calories, 150.)

You don't have to be a victim of circumstances. If there's nothing but unhealthy food in front of you, change the circumstances. Nobody forces you to eat unhealthy food. If you eat it, you do it of your own choosing. You don't have to worry about insulting anybody. You don't have to worry about going hungry. You don't have to worry about being different.

HOW TO SAY NO

Here's how to say no: You just open your mouth and articulate, *"No."*

Picture this: You're sitting in a restaurant with somebody you really like and admire. Your friend looks at the menu and orders something fried and greasy in a cream sauce and with only a trace of vitamins or minerals, if any. You're stunned. (You always thought your friend was smart!) Then *you* look at the menu and order broiled fish with no butter and a large salad with fresh lemon juice as dressing. Your friend says, "Having dessert?" You say, "No."

You've just given yourself a fabulous reward. *No* is a powerful word.

- *No,* I don't want butter on my baked potato.
- *No,* I don't want to go out for ice cream.
- *No,* I don't like fruit salad made with canned fruit, whipped cream and marshmallows.
- *No,* I don't want another helping.
- *No,* I don't want to go to a restaurant. I'd rather go with you on a walk.
- *No,* I won't skip my workout today.

A *reward* is something given or received in return or recompense for service, merit, or hardship. You actually pay yourself for saying no. You are so wise!

You're out with thin friends who are nibbling at their reuben sandwiches (the worst! Total fat, 33.3 grams; cholesterol, 77 milligrams; sodium, 1,535 milligrams; calories, 531!) and sipping sugary colas, and you have a choice. "Will it be the same for you?" asked the waitress.

"No," you say clearly. You choose a salad topped with skinless broiled chicken strips and feel smugly rewarded. "Wise choice," you smile to yourself as you chew a piece of lettuce.[1] "I'm rewarded with the joy of saying no."

You would have *punished* yourself by eating the high-sodium-fat-cholesterol sandwich. You don't deserve to be punished. You deserve to be rewarded with good things—the things that will make a happier and more beautiful you.

Listening to the Lord and obeying His voice is rewarding yourself. When you hear Him gently nudge your heart, saying, "Don't eat that," and you obey, you can sing His praises and feel wonderful. When you know in your heart He approves of a cer-

---

[1]Be sure the salad you eat includes romaine, bibb, or garden lettuce. The most popular lettuce, iceberg, contains nearly zero nutrients and is mostly water.

tain food to eat and you obey His directions, you receive a reward. Your reward is feeling good, blessed, happy, content,
pleased. You are making Jesus the Lord of your life.

PRAYER

Dear Father, I am a food addict and an abuser of my own
body. Jesus died on the cross for me to set me free from hurtful
and painful addictions. Help me to have insight into the root
causes of my addiction. Give me wisdom to understand the difference between reward and punishment. Help me to choose to
reward my body, not punish it.

I do not blame my childhood or any person for my food addiction and body abuse. I realize that nobody forces the fork into
my mouth. I do it myself. Therefore I break the hold that past
habits and experiences have had on me, tempting me to overeat
and neglect my body. In Jesus' name. Amen.

20

KNOWING THE WILL OF THE LORD

My son [or daughter], pay attention to what I say; listen closely to my words. Do not let them out of your sight, keep them within your heart; for they are life to those who find them and health to [a person's] whole body. (Proverbs 4:20–22)

The ways we abuse our bodies are endless. Food addicts and body abusers are self-destructive people who may not even realize what they are doing to themselves. By now we know that overeating and eating food high in fat, sugar, salt, and white flour are not healthy. Would you run up to someone with a highly contagious disease, such as hepatitis or mononucleosis, and shout, "Give some of that disease to me!"? How many times have you asked to borrow the toothbrush of someone with the flu?

Those examples might sound unlikely, but millions of people every day actually willingly harm their bodies. Think of the times you have made your body unhealthy. Consider the heaps of greasy food loaded with saturated fat that you've consumed in your lifetime. Think of the pounds of chocolate, the rivers of gravy and creamed soups. The average American eats 95 pounds of sugar a year, almost eight pounds every month! Our teeth, bones, liver, heart, skin, and nerves show the damage.

The Word of God leads us into health. The Word of God *is* our health. Because we love God, our love for our own bodies (the temple indwelt by the Holy Spirit) will motivate us to take better care of it.

Put away perversity from your mouth; keep corrupt talk far from your lips. (Proverbs 4:24)

The Word of God will help you speak the truth. The Word of God will show you what is corrupt and what is true.

The will of the Lord is that we live in honesty and truth. Our actions and deeds should not be hidden behind the pantry door. God's will is that our lives be pure enough not to shame us at any time.

You can shout praises to the Lord and sing, "Hallelujah, Jesus is Lord of my life!" and then minutes later steal away to the refrigerator where you slurp in half a can of Reddi-Whip squirted on your finger!

One woman shared how she sang, "Take my life and let it be, consecrated Lord to thee . . ." in the morning church service—but when she got home she ate a two-pound bag of corn chips and a bowl of guacamole. (That's 3,552 milligrams of sodium, 160 grams of fat, and 5,408 calories in the chips alone!) Because of the amount of salt she consumed, she was naturally thirsty, so she downed two cans of diet soda. (Another 72 milligrams of sodium.)

It is not God's will that we kill ourselves with a fork and spoon or straw. We were designed to eat, not to binge or starve. It is God's will that our lack of discipline be confronted. It is not God's will that we be addicted to junk food, fat- and salt-loaded foods. Some people are addicted to diet sodas or other sugared drinks. Others have their regular dose of cookies and candy bars, not unlike the drug addict hooked on drugs. One of the differences is the food junkie has a more readily available and cheaper supply at hand. They also don't have to worry about going to jail for getting caught destroying their life.

Don't be a victim of *advertising.* Our source of nutritional knowledge shouldn't come from the magazine, or TV and radio ads. If the wrapper on the bread says, "Eat this—it's good for you!" "Fat-free!" "New-light!" "Lo-Cal" *don't buy it without reading what is in it.* You decide if it's nutritious enough to eat. You decide how fat-free it is, and if your body should have it. If a product has more than 25% fat, don't buy it. Figure it out this way: 100 calories in the product should only have 2.5% fat, no more.

YOUR WILL AND GOD'S

"I've been dishonest with myself and God for years," one woman told us. "I know what it's like to *not* want to eat something and then eat it. I've even eaten things like the burnt cookies out of the batch I'm baking just because I didn't want to throw them away. I mean, they taste awful. Yet I've eaten them."

It's perverse eating when you gulp down burnt cookies as if they didn't have calories, shortening, or sugar. You are being dishonest with yourself when you lick your finger after running it over the edge of the children's sandwiches and tell yourself it doesn't matter. And when you pop the last of the food in the serving dishes into your mouth while clearing the table or scrape up the cake crumbs from around the cake and eat them, you sabotage yourself.

Three or four burnt cookies, a dollop of peanut butter and jelly, and a handful of cake crumbs could add over 25 grams of fat, 300 milligrams of sodium, and 500 calories to your daily intake! That's not even counting the sugar! The worst part is, you may not even have noticed you were eating or taking time to enjoy it!

A perverse mouth is a grumbling mouth. A perverse mouth tells lies. *The devil is a liar and the father of lies* (John 8:44). When you grumble, you are lying. You are saying things like, "*He* gets to order spareribs and I have to eat broiled fish. I'm getting the bad deal." That's a lie! He shouldn't be eating the fatty spareribs either! With 68 grams of fat in six ounces of braised lean and fat spareribs, he has just passed his maximum daily amount by eight grams. His heart doesn't need it!

The *truth* is: "Praise God, I'm eating beautiful, healthy food. My beautiful six-ounce serving of swordfish is providing me with 100 percent of my RDA of protein and has only 12 grams of fat and 280 calories. Good for me! Thank God I no longer choose to abuse my body. I can say no."

Your grateful heart won't allow your mouth to spew deceit. You won't lie, complain, or grumble. Your grateful heart swells with love and gratitude, and even if you stumble, you can say, "I'm sorry," and pick yourself up again and start anew.

You can say happily, "Lord, I love you enough to follow my daily plan. I love you and respect my body enough to exercise every day!" Make no provision for failure. You cannot lose with Jesus.

It is the will of the Lord that you succeed. It is God's will that we be wise.

We have not stopped praying for you and asking God to fill you with the knowledge of his will through all spiritual wis-

dom and understanding. And we pray this in order that you may live a life worthy of the Lord and may please him in every way: bearing fruit in every good work, growing in the knowledge of God, being strengthened with all power according to his glorious might so that you may have great endurance and patience, and joyfully giving thanks to the Father. (Colossians 1:9–12)

Meditate on the above verses. Write them in your journal. Repeat them over and over. Think about them. Paraphrase them. Think about them some more. Those words hold such magnificent promises and claims for us that we could spend a lifetime searching out their meaning and applying it to our lives.

"So that you may have great endurance and patience, and joyfully giving thanks"—what words! This tells us that becoming healthier and stronger can be a joyful thing. We're attaining steadfastness by keeping our journal and remaining faithful to our exercise plan, and by being patient as we change and grow healthier, thinner, and stronger. It's joyful!

When you are considering God's will for you, think about His *daily* will for you. What is His will for me *today*? Then, according to the above verse, as you are filled with the knowledge of His will in all spiritual wisdom and understanding, you know why obeying His will is important.

An example of a great way to set up a God's Will for Me Today Chart page is on the next page.

We know God's will by knowing His Word. The more you meditate in the Word, the more of Him—His mind, His purposes, His wisdom, His understanding, and His eternal purpose for your life—you gain.

You can't obey His will unless you *know* His will. Jesus said, "For whoever does the will of my Father in heaven is my brother and sister and mother" (Matthew 12:50). This shows us *how* close we can be to Him *if* we know His will!

We learn His will from His Word. In the Word you learn how Jesus acted, spoke, prayed, and thought. He is our model. He said, "The one who sent me is with me; he has not left me alone, for I always do what pleases him" (John 8:29). It is His will that we be pleasing to Him.

It is God's will that you gain wisdom and understanding in caring for your own body and the bodies of your loved ones.

God's Will for Me Today Chart

God's will for me today is that I	Reason:
1. Stay faithful to my commitment.	To stay in close communication with Him, so close that I control the compulsion to overeat and not exercise.
2. Be in touch with myself and my feelings.	To be honest in my actions and to understand the root causes of my food addiction and body abuse. To be unafraid to face myself and the world around me.
3. Be responsible for what I eat.	To be aware of the choices I've made in the past and to now affirm the intelligent choices I make today. I am no longer the same. I am *aware*.
4. Exercise my body.	To finally be in touch with this beautiful frame I live in. I will bless my body by exercising it and faithfully allowing it to become stronger and healthier.
5. Make sacrifices of time to have a long Daily Power Time with Him by getting up earlier, skipping a favorite TV program, making phone conversations shorter, saving magazine or newspaper reading till later.	When I miss my Daily Power Time I don't receive the strength from God I need. (When I do not read God's Word, I eat more and my life lacks power in every area.)
6. Finish a task or assignment that I've put off.	To minimize frustration. (I overeat when I'm frustrated and unfinished work that piles up frustrates me.) I feel good about myself when I accomplish what I've set out to do.
7. Do something creative that I enjoy (sewing, carpentry, pottery, painting, etc.).	To give me fun and relaxation, something I enjoy doing, and a sense of peace and self-esteem. (I tend to overeat and abuse my body when I feel bored or useless.) I think of myself as an active person.

GOD WON'T KILL US WITH FOOD

The foods that have destroyed our bodies in the past are foods that have appealed to our sensual nature, not our spirit. The Bible tells us that we are living in a world dominated by sin, but we are born-again creatures, "not of this world," and not to be *dominated* by the world of sin and its way of life.

Do you think that bag of tootsie rolls in the candy store has your name on it? Are the smells coming from that pizza restaurant calling you *personally* to their doors?

Jesus prayed to the Father not to remove those beckoning smells and sights from you, but to *keep you from succumbing to sensual, unhealthy temptations.*

> *My prayer is not that you take them out of the world but that you protect them from the evil one. They are not of the world, even as I am not of it.* (John 17:15–16)

And just when you're ready to plunge headlong into the Halloween glop in your child's trick-or-treat bag, tell yourself, "You needn't fall prey to that! Depend on the Lord *now*. He said that He has overcome. He will help me to overcome this temptation. I have the strength within me to overcome the urge to gobble up the holiday eats and candies."

Alice used to bake cookies for the family and then eat them all herself before the children arrived home from school. When the children walked in the door, they smelled the aroma of the baked cookies but found none. Alice had eaten them, crumbs and all. She had to quickly bake some extra batches in order not to face the disgrace of what she had done.

God so loved the *world*—you and me who live in the world and are living in the midst of its ways and influences—that He sent His only Son, Jesus, to die on the cross for us, and we, by believing in Him, have eternal life and power and strength to live each day above the cares of this world.

WATCH THE ADDITIVES, CHEMICALS, AND PRESERVATIVES

The world offers a lot of terrible stuff to put into your body. It even offers supposedly low-calorie products that are just as harmful to your body as sugars, fats, and processed foods. Artificial sweeteners, chemicals, additives, and preservatives have long been the outrage of health professionals who publish lengthy tomes on the dangers of these products to the human body.

Just imagine, there are 3,000 chemical additives that are permitted in processed foods! The FDA reports that the average American consumes nearly five pounds of chemicals per year! Don't you be one of them. Some of the more controversial antioxidants are these agents:

BHA (Butylated hydroxyanisole) and BHT (Butylated hydroxytoluene): Used widely in breakfast cereals, baked goods, snack foods, dry dessert mixes, beverages, shortenings, soup bases, chewing gum, and frozen meats. Laboratory animals have gotten stomach cancer from large doses.

Sodium Nitrate and Potassium Nitrate: Nearly every type of cured meat is done so with these agents. Nitrates combine with secondary amines in the stomach to form *highly carcinogenic* substances—nitrosamines. This combination is thought to have caused deaths of babies by cutting off oxygen to the brain (a condition called methemoglobinemia).

Emulsifiers, thickeners, stabilizers: These agents are close chemical relatives to soaps and detergents and are called mixing aids. They give the smooth textures to breads, puddings, ice cream, shortening, and marshmallows. *Diglycerides* are on the FDA list for a study as possibly mutagenic and having serious reproductive effects. *Calcium Sulfate,* a white, odorless, tasteless powder is used to thicken beer, wine, and baked goods. It is also known as plaster of paris and is used in cement and wall plaster as well as in some insecticides.

MSG (Monosodium Glutamate): This dangerous flavor enhancer is added to over 10,000 processed foods. It is found in nearly all convenience foods, soups, mayonnaise, snacks, crackers, packaged mixes, pickles, candies, and baked goods. It's the cause of the "Chinese Restaurant Syndrome," which includes headaches, chest pains, and numbness after eating Chinese food containing MSG. MSG has caused brain damage in rats, rabbits, chicks, and monkeys, and has been banned in all baby foods.

The All-New Free to Be Thin lifestyle plan includes healthy, fresh fruits and vegetables, whole grains, and low-fat dairy products, fish, meat, and vegetable fats. You will not be ingesting dangerous chemical additives and chemicals found in processed refined foods. No longer are you only examining the calorie content of foods, you are looking at the total picture for your total health and well-being.

We suggest that if you're accustomed to putting sugar in your hot drink, please don't switch to saccharin or a chemical sugar substitute. Try to eat more natural sugar from fresh fruit.

Be of good cheer! Feel good! You are becoming braver and wiser every day. You are becoming smarter. You know now about sugar, sweets, oils, fat—the ugly stuff meant to load your veins with cholesterol and crowd your organs with disease and fat. You're on to artificial sweetners, additives, and chemicals that deceive—not bless your delicate body.

> *For everything in the world—the cravings of sinful man, the lust of his eyes and the boasting of what he has and does— comes not from the Father but from the world. The world and its desires pass away, but the [person] who does the will of God lives forever.* (1 John 2:16–17)

You are a child of God. You are now free to eat foods that feed your body and make it strong. The Bible says the whole world lies in the power of the evil one, but you are no longer a victim of the world and its unhealthy temptations.

We are no longer ignorant of the harmful effects of sugar, sodium, and fat on our bodies. This information isn't a secret anymore. One man tells how he preached at his children about the dangers of tobacco. "Look at the warning on the wrapper," he'd tell them. Then he looked at what went into the hot dog he was eating. (He thought it was healthy because it was a chicken hot dog, but it contained 8.8 grams of fat, 45 milligrams of cholesterol, and 616 milligrams of sodium!) He realized his responsibility as a Christian is not only to be informed, but also to respond appropriately to that information.

It's a known fact that overdoses of artificial sweeteners cause cancer in laboratory animals. Extended use in the diets of children could lead to cancer in their adult years. Before you throw your hands in the air and yell, "There's not a thing a person can eat anymore! *Everything* is carcinogenic!" just look at the *huge* array of fresh foods and the delicious combination available to you.

We are not ordering you to stop eating harmful foods—but we ask you to act responsibly in light of the known facts.

You want to feel good about yourself. The Lord loves you so wonderfully. "My love and kindness shall not depart from you, nor shall My covenant of peace and completeness be removed, says the Lord, Who has compassion on you" (Isaiah 54:10, Amplified Bible).

Feel good about yourself, and don't take the fun out of eating!

PRAYER

Thank you, Lord, for the food that makes my body alive with vitality and strength. Thank you for food that builds my muscles, restores worn tissues, makes my bones, teeth, gums, hair, and skin healthy and strong.

Thank you for the power to stop lying to myself. I thank you for intelligent eating.

And I thank you, Father, for the power of your Word in my life. Thank you for your promises now coming true in my life. Thank you for your wonderful Word that has become health to my whole body, just as you said it would.

I love you!

_____

(Your name)

21

How to Get Self-control When You Don't Think You Have Any

Clarice was once a heavy smoker and smoked as many as five packages of cigarettes a day. She also had developed the habit of drinking wine every night after work. She was up to a bottle of wine a night.

When she became a Christian she gave her life to the Lord, allowing Him to work His will in her. The first thing she wanted to be free from was smoking. She still wasn't convinced the wine was hurting her, although gastric acidity and gastric irritation are a direct result of prolonged overconsumption of alcohol. Fifty percent of chronic users of alcohol have no free acid or enzymes in the stomach. Many suffer from peptic ulcers and nearly every habitual user of alcohol suffers from impaired liver function. The genito-urinary system is also affected by the use of alcohol.

Clarice marveled when the Lord helped her overcome her smoking habit. She prayed and asked Him to deliver her from cigarettes and He did. She withdrew "cold turkey" from five packs a day to none.

But drinking had become a lifestyle, and she not only enjoyed her wine, she felt she needed it.

Clarice was an addictive personality. She felt that she had no self-control whatsoever. She shared with her body buddy about her addiction to food, smoking, wine, and relationships, and she realized how much she craved acceptance and love. Her self-destructive behavior had included sickness, accidents, and unhealthy relationships with men. Clarice was faithful to attend her *Free to Be Thin* meetings and to keep in constant touch with her body buddy. She began to realize she had far more self-control than she had ever given herself credit for. She began to substitute fresh vegetable juice at night for the wine she had grown dependent upon. She also added a brisk exercise program to be done at the end of the day instead of the beginning. When she came back to her apartment every night after her long walk, she didn't feel so much like drinking. Today, Clarice has not had a drink of wine for eight years. She realizes the dangers of alcoholism and is not afraid to admit her problem. She attends meetings and is proud of her sobriety. She has also conquered her food addiction, and has lost 32 pounds and kept it off.

With the Lord's help, Clarice successfully removed three enormous strongholds in her life. She was amazed to learn how much self-control she had, because she had hidden behind the label of "addict" for too long.

Another woman had a habit of using foul language. When she overcame it she felt delighted. She was thankful she no longer cursed continually. But still she despaired over her eating habits. She believed she had absolutely no self-control.

We need to understand three things about self-control.

GOD LOVES TO GIVE GIFTS

First, God is the giver of all gifts. The fruit of self-control is one of the fruits of the Holy Spirit. You have the fruit of self-control because you have the Holy Spirit living within you.

Second, when we ask God to do something in our lives, He will do it *with our consent and effort.* (See "Your Will and God's," chapter 20.) If you ask God to get you to church on time, He can't very well do it if you don't set the alarm and get out of bed!

Self-control is saying to yourself, "Self, get out of bed."

Third, self-control is something you exercise every day of your life. In Christ, *you* are in control of your *self.* In order to read this book, you had to pick it up, you had to turn the pages, you had to put your eyes on the pages and decipher the words. You exercised *control* of your *self* and did these things. Nobody else did them for you. If someone is reading this book to you, it's *your* ears doing the listening. You are in control.

If you think you have no self-control in your life because of overeating, take a look at some other areas in your life where you do exercise self-control. Do you:

☐ Get out of bed when the alarm clock rings?

☐ Arrive at work on time?

☐ Answer the phone when it rings?

☐ Pay a bill?

☐ Make a decision about anything?

☐ Brush your teeth?

☐ Take a bath or shower?

☐ Resist the urge to do *one* thing you'd like to do, but know you shouldn't so you don't?

If you can check *yes* to any of these, you can see how you do *not* lack any self-control in your life. You're loaded with it!

List some of the bad habits and indulgences that you have already given up in your life (i.e., drugs, smoking, drinking, swearing, lying, gossiping, cheating, stealing, biting your nails, thumb-sucking, scratching, oversleeping, habitual lateness, lustful thoughts). Take time to think about the list. If you can put *one* thing on your list, you have proven that you *do* have self-control.

Now let's bring this self-control to the surface and let it work for you in the areas of your eating and exercise.

Overeating belongs in the same camp of indulgences as those on the previous list. When Clarice said, "I have victory overcoming smoking but not drinking and eating," she was not quite accurate. The truth is, she had victory in all three because they are, in fact, one area. If you can quit smoking, you can quit drinking and overeating. Some people continue to overeat because they are really *still* smoking and drinking *through* overeating.

You *do* have self-control. You're lying to yourself if you say you don't. When you read verses in the Bible that say, *"Above all else, guard your heart, for it is the wellspring of life"* and *"Let your eyes look straight ahead, fix your gaze directly before you"* (Proverbs 4:23, 25), you are reading about self-control. When you make a decision, any decision, you are exercising self-control. When you exert effort to do something that is difficult to do, you are exercising self-control.[1]

---

[1] Be sure to read *Telling Yourself the Truth* by William Backus and Marie Chapian (Minneapolis: Bethany House Publishers, 1980).

WHAT GIVES ME SELF-CONTROL

Please realize that you do have self-control. You use your self-control every day in some capacity or another. God brings self-control into your life through a variety of ways. Some of these you might not like, but some of them you will. Thank God for the privilege to learn self-control!

Psalm 119:68 says:

You are good, and what you do is good; teach me your decrees.

The way to get self-control when you don't think you have any is

1. *Realize you do have self-control.* It's simply untrue that you have no self-control. You exercise self-control every day of your life. You are exercising self-control right now by reading this book. You're telling yourself what to do and you are doing it.
2. *Stop being hard on yourself.* God knows your frame. He knows that you are a human being, endowed with human characteristics. "He looks upon the lowly," it says in Psalm 138:6. He "remembered us in our low estate" (Psalm 136:23). "The Lord protects the simplehearted; when I was in great need, he saved me" (Psalm 116:6).

David agonized in plea after plea for the Lord to rescue him from out of his troubles and weaknesses. He knew that he couldn't win any battle or overcome any struggle without the help of the Lord. He knew it because he knew that as a human being, he simply wasn't equipped to do it in his own strength.

The Lord tells us this dramatic truth: *[His] strength is made perfect in weakness* (2 Corinthians 12:9, KJV).

He shouts from heaven, *"Let the weak say, I am strong!"* (Joel 3:10, KJV).

3. *Rejoice in the self-control you do have.* Pat yourself on the back—celebrate. Every time you move the plate of cookies away from you, give yourself a warm grin, a loving nod of approval. Tell yourself, "Good for me!" Every time you order a high-fiber, low-fat meal when everyone else is eating something rich and calorie-laden, celebrate your wise choice by a long and leisurely good thought about your-

self. Every time you push yourself away from the table instead of eating dessert, rejoice. Shout a hoot of approval!

When was the last time you said, "Hurrah for me!" or "I did it!" or "Good for me!"? Start saying these things about yourself. You're terrific!

You *do* have self-control!

PRAYER

Thank you, dear Lord, for the self-control that I do have.

I now unleash the unused, God-given strength within me and call upon self-control to show itself prominently in my life.

I choose self-control in the area of food! I choose self-control over the following: (List those foods that have been your weakness.)

- _____
- _____
- _____
- _____

I choose to exercise my body daily by

- _____
- _____
- _____
- _____

Thank you that I am a person of control. I am a person of value. I am loved and doing fine. In Jesus' name I pray. Amen.

22

HOLDING ON TO THE PROMISE

Jeanette is a woman who started her program in the spring, fell off in the summer, started again in the fall, blew it at Christmas, started in January, fell off in April, started again in September—at this writing she's still going strong.

Do you see it? We are talking about a process and a journey. You don't overcome that selfish nature and those undisciplined habits overnight.

If you stumble, get up and continue on! Continue on with Jesus. Get your nose back into the Bible. Eat your spiritual life-giving food!

GET UP AGAIN

In 2 Chronicles 16, it tells how King Asa of Judah went to the king of Syria with gifts of gold and silver, pleading for his help against the king of Israel. The king of Syria obliged and conquered some of Israel's store cities in Naphtali. Then the king of Judah wiped out the work Israel was doing in building Ramah.

It looked as if King Asa really had everything going for him. He had big armies and had destroyed the enemy's stronghold. But in the middle of all his victory, God sent a prophet who told him, "You really goofed, Asa. God never intended for you to rely on some other king!"

"You mean the king of Syria whom I turned to for help?"

"That's right. God is saying, 'Because you have relied on the king of Syria and have not relied on the Lord your God, you didn't conquer what you were supposed to conquer at all.'

"Asa, listen to me," the prophet continued. "*The eyes of the Lord move to and fro throughout the earth that He may strongly support those whose hearts are completely His.* You have acted foolishly in this."

Why do we turn to fad diets, fasts, pills, drugs, shots, diuretics, liquid drinks, powdered drinks, or extreme and foolish practices to lose weight? These all fail before they begin. *God does not fail.*

Asa sounds like a familiar character. (We may wonder if he was a food abuser.) He wanted to depend on *himself* and his own ways, not on God.

What usually happens when you don't put your trust in God? If you fail, you get angry. That's what Asa did. He got furious. He threw the prophet in jail, then turned his wrath on some of the people.

He didn't want to win his battles God's way. He didn't want God's power and God's overcoming strength. He wanted *his* way. (Our way is to eat whatever and whenever we want with nobody to get in our way. Our way is to sit like a lump and never lift a finger to exercise our bodies into health.)

King Asa could have repented and started over again. But he didn't. He refused to repent. (That's what a long food binge is like. After the first 10 minutes, each additional mouthful of food is a refusal to repent.) Asa absolutely refused to admit that he was wrong and start again with the Lord.

So he failed—and failed miserably at that. He became diseased in his feet, and in verse 12 it says this disease was severe. But even *then* he wouldn't turn to the Lord for help. Do you know whom he turned to? Some physicians who couldn't help him. That's like eating arsenic when you've just swallowed cyanide.

THE TRUTH ABOUT YOU

No matter how slow your improvement is, don't give up. Even if you gain weight, don't be discouraged. Many people will lose weight and then gain some, but if you stick with *The All-New Free to Be Thin* lifestyle plan, your benefits will far outnumber any disappointment you've had.

You are at a very important place in your life. Let's take time to examine Ephesians 1:3–14 and consider *you* as God sees you:

> *Praise be to the God and Father of our Lord Jesus Christ, who has blessed us in the heavenly realms with every spiritual blessing in Christ* (verse 3).

You are blessed not only with one or two little blessings, but with *every* spiritual blessing in the heavenly places in Christ. When you're with Christ, you are in heavenly places, whether standing at the door of the refrigerator or on your knees in prayer. Your heart and your mind belong to Him to bless with *every* spiritual blessing. His spiritual blessings are eternal. They are heavenly. You are not hopeless, nor a failure in Christ. You are *blessed.*

For he chose us in him before the creation of the world to be holy and blameless in his sight (verse 4).

You are chosen! You aren't a person sitting on the fringe of the heavenly parade wishing you could be a part of it. You *are* in there! You're *chosen!*

In love he predestined us to be adopted as his sons through Jesus Christ, in accordance with his pleasure and will (verse 5).

You are adopted by Him. He has chosen you to father, to take care of, to raise and love. His intentions toward you are loving and kind.

To the praise of his glorious grace, which he has freely given us in the One he loves (verse 6).

You are lavished in His grace, in His unfailing and unmerited mercy!

In him we have redemption through his blood, the forgiveness of sins, in accordance with the riches of God's grace (verse 7).

Do you know what it is to be forgiven and made whole? Forgiven for every second and third helping your body didn't need, every gorging and binging experience? Do you know what it is to be forgiven for the causes of your overeating?

Have you prayed, "Dear Lord, *forgive* me for these feelings of frustration"? Or "Forgive me for the mistaken notion that life is passing me by, and I'm missing out on happiness and beauty"?

He lavished on us . . . all wisdom and understanding (verse 8).

You're no dummy. You have wisdom and insight! Use it!

And he made known to us the mystery of his will according to his good pleasure, which he purposed in Christ (verse 9).

If you think you just can't figure out what God's will is for you, read this verse again. He has made the mystery of His will known to us! It says so right here. Take it. Pray, "Lord, I take the power to know the mystery of your will just as it says in this ninth verse of Ephesians 1."

In him we were also chosen, having been predestined according to the plan of him who works out everything in conformity with the purpose of his will (verse 11).

That's good news! Do you know what it is to receive an inheritance? That means somebody *gives* you something; you inherit it. If you had an uncle who left you a million dollars in his will, you'd be pretty excited when that check arrived, wouldn't you? The inheritance you have in the Lord far exceeds money or riches.

In order that we, who were the first to hope in Christ, might be for the praise of his glory (verse 12).

We are the praise of His glory. You can choose to be a powerful and impressive praise to His glory. You can be a self-controlled, patient Overeater Victorious person. You can become thinner, healthier, and stronger. You can remain faithful to *The All-New Free to Be Thin* lifestyle plan, no matter how hard it seems at first.

And you also were included in Christ when you heard the word of truth, the gospel of your salvation. Having believed, you were marked in him with a seal, the promised Holy Spirit (verse 13).

You are marked forever as God's chosen one. You're *sealed* in Him. You're sealed with the Holy Spirit of promise. There's no greater gift than the Holy Spirit. He is eternal, all-powerful, all-knowing, wise, and wonderful.

Who is a deposit guaranteeing our inheritance until the redemption of those who are God's possession—to the praise of his glory (verse 14).

You are God's own possession. You're sealed by Him and you are His possession.

Reread the above verses. Write your own paraphrases and memorize them. This is your position in Christ. You are above your circumstance. You are no longer a victim of circumstances. You're blessed with every spiritual blessing in heavenly places. Ephesians 2:6 says that you are raised up with Him, seated with Him in heavenly places. You're above it all!

Start acting on who you are in Him.

WALKING WITH JESUS EVERY DAY

Here is what it might look like if we charted our daily walk with Jesus. It also would show that while we may have momentary setbacks, we are making progress over time. We are yielding every area of our life to Him, to rise above all struggles and difficulties with His overcoming wisdom and strength. We are trusting Him for all things and living as truly blessed people.

And we don't do it all in a day. Galatians 5:24 reads: "Those who belong to Christ Jesus have crucified the sinful nature with its passions and desires." This means it has been done already.

Our problem is to live like it's been done. Is that old passion of yours for ice cream or pizza still raging strong within you? This verse says if you belong to Christ, you have already crucified your old godless nature and all those old passions for destructive eating. Now the thing to do is to live like it!

PRAYER

In the name of Jesus, I renounce my old nature. The godless passions and desires in my life are no longer going to have a hold over me. I know that they are ended—crucified with Christ, because I am His! My mind is His, my will is His, my thoughts are His, my desires are His, my passions are His, my heart is His, my needs are His, my wants are His.

I am blessed with every spiritual blessing in heavenly places in Christ!

I am *chosen* in Him before the foundation of the world!

I am predestined as an *adopted* child of His!

I am lavished in His *grace*!

I have *redemption* through His blood and *forgiveness*!

I have *wisdom* and *insight* in the name of Jesus!

He has made the mystery of *His will* known to His children!

I have obtained an *inheritance* in Christ!
I am *sealed* in Him with the Holy Spirit of promise!
I am God's own possession!
In the mighty name of Jesus. Amen.

23

Have Patience With Yourself!

Larry was once a cola addict. He drank a minimum of a dozen 12-ounce cans a day. Most of the time he drank more than that. When he tried to stop, nothing seemed to work. He just couldn't break his habit. His stomach, teeth, and skin were suffering terribly. He had chronic acne, his teeth were fast decaying, and his stomach burned so badly he thought he was getting an ulcer.

Then one day he said, "That's it. This is the last cola I'm drinking," and he gave it up. It was not easy. He was like the caffeine or nicotine addict—extremely uncomfortable and irritable. He hurt from head to toe. His headaches were so severe no amount of aspirin could alleviate them. Within a week, however, he was feeling much better. He vowed to be rid of the habit forever.

A short time later he began to pray about his overeating. He began the *Free to Be Thin* program and lost nine pounds of weight the first week. The weight loss was slower after that, and one week he gained five pounds. He despaired and sank into a mood of defeat.

"But you conquered the cola habit!" the members of his group reminded him. "You're a success! You're not a failure! Why are you despairing?"

It is so easy to forget our triumphs and concentrate on failure. We need to have more patience with ourselves. Larry despaired because his eyes were focused on his weight—on the changes he was making. He measured his success by results instead of marking it by progress in changed attitudes, healthy choices, and daily quiet time insights.

God expects you to love yourself. He tells us in His Word that we are to love our neighbors as we love *ourselves*; that means we should have an abundance of healthy, sound love for ourselves first. As a result of this love, we love others with a pure and good heart. God wants you to love yourself, and because you belong to Him, you naturally want what He wants. You belong to God. You are His. You aren't something to be manipulated like a plaything.

The Lord is saying to you:

> *"So do not fear, for I am with you; do not be dismayed, for I am your God. I will strengthen you and help you; I will uphold you with my righteous right hand."* (Isaiah 41:10)

PATIENCE AND MORE PATIENCE

Patience is another fruit of the Spirit. *Be patient with yourself.* If you are patient and compassionate with yourself, you will be able to pick yourself up and start again if you stumble. You won't waste a lot of precious time in self-pity, anger, and condemnation.

You will be able to go from the **S** in struggle to the **Y** in victory without frustration and pain.

> *Therefore, there is now no condemnation for those who are in Christ Jesus.* (Romans 8:1)

Remember that!

Patience toward yourself means demonstrating mercy and compassion to yourself. You don't go all to pieces if you blow it; you ask forgiveness and start again. Patience exhibits tolerance, humility, charity, and tenderness—toward yourself as well as toward others.

Obviously one of the reasons you overeat is that you dislike yourself. You need to fight this lie by being kind to yourself. Whatever you do, reject condemnation.

WHAT TO DO WHEN YOU EAT SOME SALTY-SUGARY-SATURATED-FAT UGLY THING

It's 10:30 in the morning—and already you've eaten your daily minimum requirement of fat, you have consumed 500 milligrams of sodium, 75 percent of your daily intake of carbohydrates, and you're feeling pretty bad. Whatever you do, don't tell yourself you'll go back on your program tomorrow: *Do it at lunch!* Keep track of your fat grams, carbohydrates, protein, fiber, and sodium intake. Make sure you have some fruit!

Don't skip meals to try to atone for your sins.

Jesus Christ is our atonement for sins. You can't atone for them. On *The All-New Free to Be Thin* lifestyle plan you are learning how to *eat,* not diet. You are not in prison here. You've been set free from the prison of your own self-destruction.

It may take some struggles and a few ups and downs, but it's all in the process of understanding yourself better and developing your self-control. You're making progress, be assured of that, though sometimes the going gets a little choppy.

If your motive is only to lose weight, you could eat paper for a month and that would do the trick. But your motives are higher than that. You want health, wholeness, freedom—*life.* If you are obsessed with losing weight, you never seem to lose it as fast as you wish you could. Those great claims made by promoters of fad diets or weight-loss spas and clinics—telling you that in one month you'll be 30 pounds thinner, or that by Christmas, the Fourth of July, your birthday, Aunt Maude's housewarming, or your own wedding day, you'll be a sliver of your former chubby self—are not only unsound, but unhealthy. We said earlier that you shouldn't fast to lose weight when you are in the process of learning how to *eat.* What you are learning now is consistency and good daily habits.

Food abusers often choose radical weight-loss methods that harm their bodies and destroy their health because of a mistaken notion that doing something radical will somehow atone for the "sins" which caused them to be fat. Selfishness makes patience hard to come by.

A Promise With a Hollow Ring to It

If slimness is your only goal and you want to be 30 pounds slimmer *now,* you're going to be a sitting duck for the countless weight-loss hypes. When some scheme comes along, promising you that you can lose a pile of weight in a short time, you're going to reach into your pocket and pay whatever they ask to have this dream come true in your life.

The sad thing is, the dream doesn't come true. You may lose weight and a lot of money, but statistics have shown the weight doesn't stay off. Don't be like one pathetic woman we know who drank predigested liquid protein and lost 65 pounds, but damaged her heart and metabolism, so that she may never be normal again.

Jesus knows about your addiction to food and the abuse you have done to your body. He carried your troubles and problems on himself when He went to the cross so that you could be free *now.*

But "now" takes patience.

> *No discipline seems pleasant at the time, but painful. Later on, however, it produces a harvest of righteousness and peace for those who have been trained by it. Therefore, strengthen your feeble arms and weak knees. Make level paths for your feet, so that the lame may not be disabled, but rather healed.* (Hebrews 12:11–13)

Maybe this is the first time in your life you've had an opportunity to learn how to be patient with yourself, kind to yourself, gentle to yourself, merciful toward yourself. It is God's will that you have mercy on yourself. "I will have mercy and not sacrifice," He tells us.

You need patience toward yourself to be a successful Christian. You need it so that if you make a mistake, you don't hate and then punish yourself by making destructive choices. Instead, you have mercy on yourself.

PRAYER

I am a born-again child of God. Thank you, Father, for your great love and mercy. Thank you for sending Jesus to die on the cross so that I don't have to atone for my own sins.

Thank you for your Holy Spirit enabling me to have mastery over my weaknesses. I refuse to be a selfish person. *I have self-control.*

Thank you for developing patience in me. Thank you, Lord, for showing me how I sabotage my own happiness. I can be patient, kind, and understanding toward myself!

Thank you, Lord, that you do not expect me to conquer all my faults in one day. I am not discouraged at my progress because you are with me. In Jesus' name. Amen.

24

WHY DO YOU ABUSE YOUR BODY?

Have you ever thought your eating disorder was unique and separate from the rest of the people in the world? If your thin friends had the life of troubles that you had, they'd gain weight, too, you think. If the rest of the world suffered as you do, they'd be sick, too.

Have you ever thought that nobody hurts like you do? This way of thinking says everybody has a happier and better life than you and overeating is all you've got. The notion that others are happier, better off, and leading lives of comparative ease is not true at all. All who have ever attempted any lifestyle change have had to struggle with temptation, deny themselves, and go without.

That's what the Word tells us. In 1 Corinthians 10:13 it says:

No temptation has seized you except what is common to man.

This verse says that we are in the human realm of existence, and the problems that beset us are all within this human realm. There's no superhuman task facing us. That's why the Lord tells us in Matthew 17:20 that if we have faith as a mustard seed, nothing is impossible for us.

There is not a single temptation that is beyond what we can handle with God's help.

And God is faithful; he will not let you be tempted beyond what you can bear. But when you are tempted, he will also provide a way out so that you can stand up under it.

With the temptation, God always provides a way of escaping its power over you so that you may endure and not fall. The reason many of us don't grab hold of this promise is that we want to be excused from our Christian responsibility to think and act like Christians.

WHAT MAKES US DO IT?

Have you become angry with anyone or anything lately? Have you been upset, worried, furious, miserable, frustrated, depressed, or anxious with anyone or anything?

Have you ever noticed the way children behave when they've been caught doing something they shouldn't be doing? One of the first things they might say is that someone else made them do it. Two small boys invade the cookie jar and when Mother happens on the scene, they both point at the other and say in harmony, "*He* made me do it!"

It's the mature person who can stop blaming people and situations for his/her own problems. The responsibility for our happiness is on our own shoulders. Nobody else holds it for us. We do.

People don't actually *make* you angry. You make yourself angry. Imagine driving in your car with a friend. This friend is telling you every turn and stop to make, as if you had never been behind a wheel before. He is being a backseat driver *par excellence.*

You think to yourself, *This guy is really making me angry. In a minute I'll explode.*

Explode you may, but not because he makes you angry. You may want to throw your Indie 500 trophy at him, as well as your international chauffeur's license, but please, as you do, say the truth and tell him, "I *make myself* angry when you tell me how to drive."

Nobody else *makes* you do anything. You make *yourself* feel, think, say, act, and do what you do. Nobody else actually makes you overeat. You overeat because of you.

You *condition* yourself to eat what you eat, where you eat, how much you eat, and when you eat.

WHAT IT MEANS TO BE CONDITIONED

If you have had several happy experiences eating and watching TV, you will have an automatic trigger inside your brain telling you to *eat* when you get in front of the TV. You only need to see a TV set turned on and you'll feel like eating something. If you have paperwork to do and you've conditioned yourself to eat while working, you'll find yourself thinking of food as you work. If you have made a habit of eating when you're depressed, upset, lonely, or worried, your brain will tell you *eat* when you are in that state of mind. You've conditioned yourself to eat when you encounter these stressful circumstances.

Now, here's the good news. You can be renewed, reconditioned in your mind. You can develop new habits so that your brain does not think *food* when you are in certain situations or places or engaging in certain activities. One woman says that she doesn't overeat at all during the day when she is on the job, but the minute she walks into her apartment, she starts to eat and doesn't stop until she goes to bed.

Somewhere along the line she conditioned herself to think food and home are inseparable. On the job she didn't think about eating, but once home, her "eat" trigger was pushed and off she went, eating everything in sight.

Home should not mean food to us. Home is a million things, and eating is only one of the things we do there. The experiences as a child when Mother cooked up those feasts in her kitchen and all the family rallied around the table for family time, with food as the main attraction, may still remain in your memory. So you spend your years trying to relive these childhood experiences. Or maybe food means relaxation to you. When you arrive home after a day of pressure and hard work, you want to relax. Relaxation means food, so you not only eat, but you overeat.

You can end these lifetime patterns and develop new ones.

Check if you do any of the following:

- [ ] Eat while watching TV
- [ ] Eat while driving the car
- [ ] Eat while studying or doing paperwork
- [ ] Eat while reading
- [ ] Eat while on the job
- [ ] Eat while shopping
- [ ] Eat while preparing a meal
- [ ] Eat when cleaning up after a meal
- [ ] Eat more alone than with others
- [ ] Eat before going to bed
- [ ] Get out of bed in the middle of the night to eat
- [ ] Eat more on weekends than during the week
- [ ] Eat more at night than during the day
- [ ] Skip breakfast but gorge later on in the day

Renewing must begin with the strength of God's Word (Your

Daily Power Time), then reconditioning can help you make the changes in lifestyle you desire so much. Many times change comes by conciously *choosing* a different course or path—a different activity such as:

Don't eat while watching TV. Do your nails, sew, whittle, carve, or paint something instead.

Don't eat while driving the car. Wait until you get to a restaurant, home, or wait until a certain time.

Don't eat while studying or doing paperwork. A glass of beautiful water will be terrific.

Don't eat while reading. Be good to yourself. Enjoy your book without abusing your body.

Don't eat while on the job. Wait until lunch or dinner and reward yourself with a fitness break.

Don't eat while shopping. Your body will love you for it.

Don't eat while preparing a meal. Your body doesn't want you to put more into it than it needs.

Don't eat while cleaning up after a meal. You are not a garbage disposal; you are a beautiful human being.

Don't eat more alone than when you're with others. Be good to yourself at all times, not just in front of others.

Don't get out of bed in the middle of the night to eat. Your stomach deserves a rest.

Don't eat before going to bed. Instead, think lovely, restful thoughts. Take a wonderful "air bath" for your lungs.

Don't eat more on weekends than during the week. Discover your "triggers" and put an end to them.

Don't eat more at night than during the day. Do something fun like your stretches instead of eating.

Don't skip breakfast and gorge at other times. Breakfast is energy time. You are too special to go without your morning energy. Don't forget to eat six times a day: three meals and three healthy snacks.

You may have a string of excuses for overeating and abusing your body, but you can change these. God is showing you the root of your body-abuse problems. Don't be afraid to face yourself.

PRACTICAL HELPS FOR THOSE TOUGH TIMES OF TEMPTATION

1. Tell your friends you're changing your eating lifestyle when they invite you for a meal. Tell them exactly what

you *may* eat and what you may not. They may even become educated and decide to change their own eating habits to be more health conscious.

2. When you eat in a restaurant, plan what you'll order before you get there. Think of the many lovely foods you can choose from. Steamed vegetables, a huge vegetable salad, potato, rice, broiled poultry, fish, fresh fruit—don't use eating out as an excuse to hurt yourself. Avoid looking at a menu whenever possible.

3. If others want to eat unhealthy foods, you don't have to join them. You eat your nutritious and beautiful salad and broiled fish, or whatever you choose from the endless array of possibilities, and thank Jesus you've taken the way of escape.

4. Become familiar with which foods contain the most fat, sodium, cholesterol, chemicals, and additives. Just the mention of an Italian sausage should remind you right away of harmful nitrates, too much fat (17.2 grams in a tiny two-ounce link), high cholesterol (52 milligrams, to be exact), and way too much sodium (believe it or not, 618 milligrams!). As you familiarize yourself with foods, it will be easier for you to shop, eat in restaurants, and prepare meals at home.

5. Stay away from junk foods when you're shopping. Don't buy prepared meals. Don't buy frozen dinners. If your family insists on these foods, let someone else buy them. One woman told her husband, "Your snacks and junk foods will have to come out of the entertainment money because my grocery money must go for *food*."

6. Cut up carrots, celery, and cauliflower immediately and keep in a plastic container in the refrigerator to have some ready, healthy "fast food" on hand.

7. At church dinners, potlucks, showers, weddings, and other food-oriented activities, you bring some nutritious and scrumptious eats like fresh fruit with lemon dressing, cold sliced turkey breast or crisp vegetable salad. Bring a thermos of herb tea or your wonderful bottled water.

8. Cut back on sweets and choose natural sweeteners whenever possible. Eat plenty of fresh fruit. Using artificial sweeteners saves calories but does nothing to help retrain taste and habits. Before buying or eating, you need to think

about the effects of anything artificial going into your precious body.

You are a unique and special person—a very important person. You deserve to have good things. Those good things do *not* include harmful foods.

You are unique as a person created with God's very own mind. He loves your soul, your spirit, *and your* body. He knows your body. He formed you. It's important to Him that it operate and function well.

For you created my inmost being; you knit me together in my mother's womb. I praise you because I am fearfully and wonderfully made; your works are wonderful, I know that full well. My frame was not hidden from you when I was made in the secret place. When I was woven together in the depths of the earth. (Psalm 139:13–15)

NUTRITION AND MENTAL HEALTH

What you eat plays an important role in your emotional state of being. You may be consuming huge amounts of food, but if you are not getting the vitamins and minerals your body requires according to your lifestyle, metabolism, and body needs, you will suffer for it.

If you are subject to periods of depression, mental confusion, and other emotional deviations for which you find no psychological cause, you may want to examine your diet. Evaluate what you are eating and see if you are consuming a high-carbohydrate, high-fiber, low-sodium, lower-protein diet necessary for optimum mental stability. Are you getting enough B vitamins (tension reducing), potassium (easily excreted during stress periods), and magnesium (vital for control of muscle tension and irritability)?

Processed cereals, white flour, and white sugar do not offer the complete range of B vitamins necessary to promote adequate food metabolism. Coffee and other caffeine beverages stimulate the insulin production and cover up fatigue. Avoid them because they hide the symptoms of low blood sugar and detract its cure.

Connie gorged on chocolates after her divorce and put on 15 pounds. Tom wolfed down fat and sugar-laden treats and gained 20 pounds when he lost his job. Marsha took to constant nibbling after the birth of her second child. Darlene ate cookies and nuts at her desk at work and gained weight, becoming more lethargic each day.

For these people a specific event in their life had triggered their desire to eat. Upon talking with each of them, it was unanimous that none of them were even aware when they were overeating. Connie said, "I just slip into sort of an empty vacuum when I pig out."

It's time to face your disappointments with life, the hurts you experience, and the frustrations and sorrows of the present and the past.

PRAYER

Dear Lord, please continually show me the root of my body abuse and food addiction. Thank you for the long way I've already come. Thank you for loving me enough to be at my side every step of the way. My health is in your hands. In Jesus' name. Amen.

25

"There's More to Being Thin Than Being Thin" Maintenance for Life

It is for freedom that Christ has set us free. Stand firm, then, and do not let yourselves be burdened again by a yoke of slavery. (Galatians 5:1)

The Greatest Victory

What could be better than being healthy? Now you've arrived—you've reached your health and fitness goal and you're ready to take *The All-New Free to Be Thin* lifestyle plan with you for the rest of your life. In our book *There's More to Being Thin Than Being Thin*,[1] we tell the stories of some of the thousands of people who have lost weight on the Overeaters Victorious *Free to Be Thin* program. We discovered several years ago after the enormous success of the *Free to Be Thin* plan that there really is more to being thin. Countless men and women have discovered the spiritual benefits this program encourages. That's why we call maintenance *"more."*

When you didn't exercise and when you were a victim of your overeating habits, you were in bondage. Now you're free. Overeating for whatever reason you can think of is *bondage.* It's like being in a prison or being wrapped in heavy chains from head to toe. You're trapped like a slave, unable to move in freedom. Binging and gluttony are your slave drivers. They crack the whip and you jump like a beaten slave. Whatever emotion you blame your overeating on, you are a slave to it. You may say, "Oh dear, I'm feeling depressed. I want to *eat* a little something."

---

[1]*There's More to Being Thin Than Being Thin* by Neva Coyle and Marie Chapian (Minneapolis: Bethany House Publishers, 1984).

Or, "How dare he speak to me that way! He doesn't love me. Nobody loves me. I'm all alone in this life, loveless and lonely. I think I'll eat."

Now that you've reached the "There's More" Maintenance Program, you have arrived home at last. Your body has finally emerged healthier, fit, and strong. The real you has burst through those prison walls. Thank God, you're free! It was for the sake of freedom that your Savior set you free. Praise God, keep standing firm! Don't go back to that ugly prison again!

You have victoriously feasted on Jesus and His Word. The real you is now reading these words. Those hands of yours are no longer swollen and bulging around your rings, your breathing is easier, and you aren't gasping for breath. Your clothes fit. You feel great!

ARE YOU READY FOR MORE?

You go on the "There's More" Maintenance Program when you reach the *spiritual* goals God has set for you. This is the point where you are utterly honest with the Lord in your life. You no longer hide foods from the Lord. You don't miss your Daily Power Time, you fight those things that trigger gluttonous eating, you stop complaining about not being able to eat certain foods, you exercise *regularly,* and you remain faithful to your calling and God's will for your body.

If you are still having temper tantrums and going on weekend binges, if you're still sitting instead of walking, you aren't ready for the "There's More" Maintenance Program quite yet. *You want to maintain the good work God has done in you for the rest of your life.*

THE PURPOSE OF THE "THERE'S MORE" MAINTENANCE PROGRAM

The reason we go on the maintenance program is so that God can continue to move in us as He desires. God has a lot He wants done in our lives and He wants to get on with it! The longer you sit in fleshly indulgences, self-pity, anger, overeating, gluttony, binging, gorging, eating wrong foods, and no exercise, the longer it takes Him to get on with the other wonderful things He has for you in your life! *Don't miss out!*

Maintaining healthy habits, good food choices, and fitness

routines is the way *you* keep control of your actions and open the way for God to meet your desires for freedom.

Now is the time for you and your body buddy to celebrate with a great big glass of beautiful water and to do something fun like a new sport together. (How about roller-blading? Okay. Then how about a brisk hike through a beautiful nature park?) You now have self-control! A person with self-control is ready to go on to enjoy more wonderful blessings from feeling healthy and fit.

"But how do I know what to eat?" you may ask. You *do* know what to eat. You have been on the program, listened to the voice of the Lord, and been in the Word long enough to know very well what to eat and what not to eat. *Stand firm and do not be subject again to a yoke of slavery.* You are now accustomed to saying no to temptation and failure. You have studied foods and labels, you know fat, sodium, and sugar contents in foods, and you are exercising regularly. You are saying *yes* to the Holy Spirit as He guides you in godly eating and exercise.

God is saying to you, "You know now what your body needs. You have worked hard to get where you are. Good job! Keep it up! There are blessings ahead you haven't even imagined."

The reason you are on the maintenance program now is that you *do* understand yourself and your body and you are in *control.* Imagine spending several weeks teaching a child how to ride a bicycle. He falls a few times, makes some errors, but finally, he does very well. He gains coordination and stays up on the bicycle. You can see that he has learned how to ride well. Then you tell him, "Okay, you're ready to go on that bike trip."

He answers, "But how do I ride the bike?"

You answer, "I taught you how to ride. You know how to ride. All you have to do is *do it* now."

"But how do I do it? What do I need to know in order to ride the bicycle?"

"I already told you everything you need to know. You already showed me that you know how to ride the bike. You are prepared. Go ahead."

The reason God wants you to act on what you know is that He wants to teach you something new! He doesn't want you in the same old ruts forever. You have learned much about yourself and your body. Now go on! He has *much more* for you!

Every day when you get out of bed, ask the Lord what new things He has in store for you. Give Him your day and every morsel of food you'll be putting in your mouth. Give Him your body for exercise.

You're on the "There's More" Maintenance Program and all the more reason to *stand firm.* Pie should be no less disgusting to you now than it was when you started getting healthy, losing weight, and becoming stronger. Neva didn't taste ice cream for two years.[2] "This is a lifetime thing," she explains. "Things like candy and ice cream are no friends of mine. They aren't *treats* either, I'll tell you that. I don't consider cakes and cookies *refreshments* anymore. These foods are threats to my health and well-being. I choose to stand firm and not be subject again to the yoke of slavery these kinds of 'refreshments' and 'treats' once had on me. My treats are now healthy, life-giving foods, the kind my body loves, like fresh fruit, yogurt, raw vegetables, and fresh juices."

You will have a closer awareness of yourself through your journal.

Continue to keep a very close log of your feelings, moods, and behavior. Make your journal entries longer and spend more time in the Scriptures. The reason for this is that you need to have a thorough awareness of yourself—your desires, thoughts, wants, dreams, emotions, and actions. Leave nothing to chance. It is not by chance you are where you are now.

In order to make your "There's More" Maintenance Program a living reality and the joy it ought to be, go back frequently to making out a Desire-Action Worksheet. Write your desires and the actions you are taking to fulfill these desires. Your desire is now to maintain your new habits. What are you doing about it?

Apply this to other areas of your life.

Here is what one woman on the maintenance program wrote:

---

[2]Have you been telling yourself that ice cream is nutritious because it's a supposed milk product? Here are just a few of the more than 60 chemical additives that might be inside your favorite ice cream: carrageenan, furcelleran, agar-agar, alcin, calcium sulfate, gelatin, gum karaya, locust bean gum, oat gum, gum tragacanth, mono- and diglycerides, polysorbate 65 and 80, sodium carboxymethylcellulose, popylene glycol alginate, microcrystalline cellulose, dioctyl sodium sulfoscuccinate, sodium citrate, disodium phosphate, tetrasodium pyrophosphate, sodium hexametaphosphate, calcium carbonate, magnesium additives. These are used to stimulate flavor, color, texture and to prevent crystal formation during storage. Ice cream does not list ingredients on the package. If you're still singing "Ice cream, ice cream, we all scream for ice cream," it's time to scream, "No!" This high-calorie dessert, loaded with fat, sugar, and cholesterol, just isn't worth singing about.

DESIRE	ACTION
Stop yelling at the kids.	Begin each day praying for each of them. Choose a special scripture verse for each and repeat these throughout the day in order to be thinking God's thoughts about my children instead of my own, which may be hurtful and selfish.

Go to bed early so I am rested.

Be certain their duties are clearly understood and make them aware of the consequences if they do not complete these when expected. This will eliminate my hollering at them and getting myself upset.

Pay careful attention to our diet so we are getting plenty of the B vitamins (necessary for healthy nerves). Add more calcium, too.

Meditate on what Jesus would do if He were in my shoes. What is His thinking on this? How does He feel about my children and about our situation? He wouldn't yell. What *would* He do?

This is also a good time for you to do your *God's Will for Me Chart* again. You don't want to neglect these practices in your life. You should make these charts continually throughout your life in order to keep close contact with *yourself.* In Christ, you can choose to have control of your life. These are some tools to help you stay in control. You stay in control by keeping close contact with yourself, your feelings, and your actions. Your journal is of vital importance at this point.

Reach out with your new self-control in other areas of your life. You have self-control in your eating and you'll have it in other areas, too.

SOME TEMPTATIONS WHEN GOING ON THE "THERE'S MORE" MAINTENANCE PROGRAM

You probably won't be tempted to overeat as you once were, but you may encounter the temptation to relax your resolutions to avoid fat and sugar. You may be tempted to say things like:

"Oh, one little piece of _____ (fattening, unhealthy food) won't hurt me. After all, I'm at my goal weight now."

"What's one helping of _____ (fattening, unhealthy food). One helping won't hurt me."

"Maybe if I go off my program just this *once*—"

"I deserve a _____ (fattening, unhealthy food) for working so hard."

Don't forget that it was that table loaded with cakes and cookies, that bakery window, the ice cream parlor, those desserts, gravies, rich and fattening foods that once tempted you to the point your body became victimized! Do you want to become prisoner to these foods again? *It was for freedom that Christ set you free; therefore keep standing firm and do not be subject again to a yoke of slavery.*

Make a list of the "yokes of slavery" that once held you bound. Include the reasons you overate, also. Then write how Jesus has healed the hurts that motivated you to eat.

The truth is: One little piece of that fattening and unhealthy food will not ruin your life. But *be aware. Be in control.* You control food; food does not control you.

The only food you deserve is the food that blesses your body and soul. The food you deserve is good, wholesome, healthy food that will make your body run the best it possibly can. You deserve the best! You are a very special child of God and you don't deserve junk for that beautiful body of yours, not even one little bite. You worked hard to make the progress you've made. You deserve the best!

PRAYER

Father, in the name of Jesus, I am free because Jesus has set me free. I am standing firm. I will not be subject again to a yoke of slavery.

I am no longer a slave of anger, revenge, frustration, loneliness, nervousness, worry, or boredom.

I no longer eat to reward myself.

I no longer eat for comfort.

I no longer eat for "treats."

I am no longer a slave to other people's eating habits. I no longer eat unhealthy and fattening foods to please others or to avoid hurting their feelings.

I eat according to the Word of God—to glorify God in my body.

I make these statements in the name of Jesus Christ, my Lord and Savior, who redeemed me from sin and death by His own death on the cross. His blood was shed for me so that I can be free to love Him and serve Him with my whole body, soul, and spirit.

I thank you, Father, in the name of Jesus, that I am free from overeating, free from gluttony, free from binging, free from lethargy and achy, unused muscles.

Thank you for my maintenance program, which I begin in the name of Jesus and for your glory. Amen.

I Am Victorious

Today, I walk in victory. I am totally victorious over food. I do not abuse food or use it for satisfaction, reward, or emotional outlet. I do not express my anger or frustration by overeating.

Jesus satisfies me. He gives me strength to handle anger and frustration, and to live up to my daily responsibilities. I take responsibility for my choices. I have learned how to reward myself for making good choices. I do not live in denial. I can face my problems and work at resolving them with the Lord as my Helper. He rewards me with love, encouragement, and the good life.

I worship God today in praise, obedience, and positive attitudes. Because He loves me, I can love and respect myself. I am entitled to the best of life because Jesus died to give it to me.

The Holy Spirit gives me the strength to refuse the foods that hurt my body, and helps me to stop eating enormous quantities of food. The Holy Spirit helps me and reminds me of the happiness I feel when I exercise my body.

I belong to God completely. I do not surrender to junk foods and lack of exercise. I choose to live my life in the Spirit of God.

26

Keeping What's Yours

Never Let It Go—It's Yours!

You will maintain your goals of healthy food choices and fitness forever when you keep a continual guard over your mouth, your appetite, and your exercise commitment. You can't assume for a minute that because you have reached your goals, you can relax and set your armor down. You may want to say, "But when do I get to stop being the perpetual soldier in the battlefield of life?"

The good news is that it's never too difficult for you to be in the army of God. He will never forsake you because He's in the frontlines right beside you. *He's the winner at all times.*

So many people who have reached their goals on *The All-New Free to Be Thin* lifestyle plan have told us, "I can't get over how much energy I've got. When I was overeating, sick, and weak, I never had energy. I could hardly walk without losing my breath, my legs ached, my ankles were constantly swollen, my feet hurt, and I always felt tired."

Never let it go!

Here are Mr. and Mrs. Overcomer. They are standing at the threshold of their new home, which they have been building the last months. It's a lifetime dream come true. They've always wanted a new house. The decorating and finishing is complete and they are ready to move in. They are so happy they want to jump for joy.

As they stand admiring the beautiful construction and finishing touches of the house, they see a storm heading their way.

They get inside the house just before the sky rips open and wind and rain assail the neighborhood. What do Mr. and Mrs. Overcomer do next? As the storm rages outside, instead of closing all windows and doors, they suddenly open them. They throw open the front door, the back doors, patio doors, and garage doors.

Then they watch as the rain ruins the wallpaper, carpeting, and floors, and they cry, "Oh, poor us. Everything happens to us!" Then they drag their furniture outside and set it in the mud, crying, "Isn't this awful! Even our furniture is getting ruined in this storm."

Farfetched? Not really. Look at yourself for a moment. You now have a new body. You're healthy and gorgeous for Jesus. Your body is your beautiful new home, and you've worked hard for it. When storms of temptation come your way, what are you going to do? Are you going to open the doors and windows of your heart and mind for the storms to ruin? Are you going to let temptations damage any part of your beautiful new self?

Not you!

If Mr. and Mrs. Overcomer really love their new home, they'll protect it. They'll make sure it is built so well that it will withstand storms. They'll take care of the house and make sure it is in good shape at all times. It's important because they have a big investment.

Your investment is even bigger. You've invested your life. If your home were to be destroyed, your body would not necessarily die because of it. You could go on living, although you'd have to find another home. But this isn't true with your body. If your body is destroyed, where else can you move? It's shocking how many people take better care of their houses than their precious bodies.

God has an investment in you, too.

> When a strong man, fully armed, guards his own house, his possessions are safe. But when someone stronger attacks and overpowers him, he takes away the armor in which the man trusted and divides up the spoils. (Luke 11:21–22)

THE GOOD BATTLE

Your battle is not with the Twinkie or the Oreo cookie. It's not the cheesecake that hammers on your taste buds and screams, "Eat! Eat!" It's not the recliner chair that keeps you from using the Stairmaster. It's not the sofa that holds you down, preventing you from letting the stationary bike build you up.

Gorgeous person, you *need* the full armor of God (see Ephesians 6:13–18). How do you put on His armor? It's relatively simple. You stay completely honest with the Lord. You remain in complete and continual communication with Him. You are truthful about your feelings, your emotions, and your needs. If you need love and attention, don't deny it or deny yourself. If you are angry inside, look at your anger, discuss it with someone (a licensed Christian counselor or therapist can help enormously) and deal with it. Reach out—your needs are important.

You are surrounded with the love of God. He is the author of truth and freedom.

Connect yourself to heaven on a direct wire that buzzes regularly with the sound of your prayers. Talk continually to Him. Praise Him, worship Him. Keep your nose in the Word. And listen when He speaks to you.

Put on the full armor of God. Now, why does a person always have to wear the full armor of God? Isn't that tiring? Boring? I mean, don't you think a person could find better things to do?

No, a person couldn't do anything more worthwhile. Healthy person, don't just put on the armor of God. Put on the *full* armor of God—all of it. Cover up, zip up, snap in, button on, hook together, tie yourself snugly; no holes, leaks, tears, or rips in the full armor of God. Satan's schemes are to steal your victory and make you miserable. He hates God and he hates you. He wants to wreck anything that glorifies God. He'd like to break every bone in your body—destroy you completely. He'd like to turn you into dust and get you to curse God. He hates it that you're not overeating and hurting your body and soul. He hates it that you *like* yourself now.

Galatians 6:9 says, "Let us not become weary in doing good, for at the proper time we will reap a harvest if we do not give up." Read that verse and then tell yourself, *"Self, don't lose heart in doing good. You've been terrific so far. Now, don't you get discouraged. Your proper time for rewards and a healthy life is here. Don't be weary now, of all times. You made it! Your body is submitted to God! You've obeyed, you've remembered your commitment, and you've worked out faithfully. Now you have a new body of health and vitality to glorify the Lord in. Praise God for the wisdom you have chosen and for the fact that you have not given up!"*

Love yourself. Love your wisdom and your integrity. Love your new choices. Love your new life. You are no longer a chump for a plateful of cookies. Your tastes have changed. You're eating fiber and green, leafy vegetables. You're delighting in fresh fruits and wonderful water. You're aware of the importance of complex carbohydrates. You have learned a new way to cook. You love life!

YOUR "THERE'S MORE" DAILY POWER TIME

You need your Daily Power Time like you need air to breathe and water to drink. You need it like you need rest and food. Wear righteousness like integrity. That's what Ephesians 6 talks about. Righteousness and integrity.

When you are ready spiritually to go on the "There's More" Maintenance Program, you are no longer *developing* good eating and exercise habits; you're *living* them.

You're no longer stumbling around confused or bewildered about a healthy lifestyle. You're walking in the Spirit now! You're wise, able to make fine choices! You're good to yourself.

Can you praise the Lord right now as you are reading this and thank Him for your new life! You are a partaker of His divine nature!

Every day when you have your Daily Power Time and you pray to the Lord about your appetite and your exercise routine, you are proving your commitment to Him. The Lord loves your faith. *It's impossible to please Him without faith* (Hebrews 11:6). When you trust Him to help you with your problem of overeating and lack of an effective workout program, you are showing faith that He indeed *will* help.

The cry of so many body abusers is, "How can I be a good example and a witness for Jesus when I'm so undisciplined? How can I tell people that Jesus will help them with their problems when my own problems are so obvious?" That fear is probably one of the reasons you violated your health and body in the first place. When you violate your body you violate your soul. It works the other way, too. Do you think you have to be *perfect* before you can help someone else who also is not perfect? We are all in this human lifeboat together. It is not horrible to have problems. It is not the end of the world to be imperfect.

Denying our problems or repressing them can have awful effects on our lives. Admit your problem. Face it. "I am a food abuser, but I am getting better" are the words to use during *The*

All-New Free to Be Thin lifestyle plan. Now that you are on your way to a healthier, happier, controlled lifestyle, you can say, "I am not perfect, but God has shown me how to overcome many of my problems. I have abused food and used it for comfort and fullness, and it never gave me the comfort and fullness I craved. I have violated myself by not exercising my body and now I have learned a new lifestyle. I am here to tell you about it if you would like to hear what God has done for me."

Jesus heals us of our diseases, delivers us from ruin, and is the Savior of mankind. He saves us from overeating and destroying ourselves if we let Him. Your Daily Power Time will show you more and more of the mercies of God. Morning by morning you will see and know more of His mercy. Have mercy on yourself. You're beautiful!

THE HOLY STOPLIGHT

Jeanne had lost 52 pounds on the *Free to Be Thin* program, and was now working hard to change her exercise habits. It was important to her to exercise and she had learned the joy of working out her body. One Saturday morning she was driving in her car to do some errands when she saw a half-eaten bag of salty, greasy tortilla chips on the seat beside her. She had not eaten breakfast. (This is a setup for failure: *Always eat breakfast.*) So she absently reached over and began nibbling on them. She thought, "Oh well, I haven't had breakfast. Just one little bite will give me some energy."

Energy is *not* what she got. After she had polished off the bag, her appetite was geared up so high she could have eaten Tucson. She decided she would just stop at the fast-food restaurant on the corner and have a little bite of breakfast.

A "little bite." For the overeater and food abuser, a "little bite" has an entirely different meaning than it does for the non-food abuser. She was practically breathless when she got to the restaurant. She knew what was on the menu and remembered those photographs of disgusting foods. Suddenly, she remembered a story of a woman in the *Free to Be Thin* book who had the same experience but stopped herself before the binges. She remembered the Bible verse, "I can do everything through him who gives me strength" (Philippians 4:13). She stopped at the door.

What triggered her urge to binge? The chips she ate? "No," says Jeanne, "I felt lonely, overwhelmed, and in need of *filling* myself. I had worked hard all week and I was still working hard on Saturday morning. I was hungry because I hadn't eaten yet and I wanted the feeling of *fullness*."

Jeanne called her body buddy from the pay phone outside the restaurant. She met her friend at the health club. Even though Jeanne didn't have her workout clothes with her, she and her body buddy worked out on the stationary bikes for half an hour, then later enjoyed her favorite carrot-apple juice at the health bar. They then prayed and read the Scriptures to each other (see chapter 18).

"I was filled, really. I am learning every day to recognize those triggers that would cause me to punish and hurt myself by abusing my body."

Soak yourself in the Word of God so that the magnificent, holy words will hold you tightly and guard you from falling prey to your emotions.

PRAYER

Dear Jesus, I choose to allow nothing to interfere with my relationship with you and the teaching you have brought into my life regarding eating and exercise. I choose to completely cover myself in the armor of God so that I am able to resist temptation, understand my emotions, and stand my ground. I choose to keep alert to my feelings and to pray at all times. I love you! Amen.

27

HOW TO TALK ABOUT BEING HEALTHY WITHOUT BEING AN UNBEARABLE BORE

What could be worse than being excited about something, sharing it with your friends, and discovering they aren't fascinated? You may wonder, What's wrong with everybody? Why aren't they intrigued when I tell them what I had for lunch? Where is the drum roll when I talk about how I always cut off all the skin and fat from my broiled chicken and never, no *never,* eat my veggies with butter or margarine?

Why doesn't everybody else hear the same heavenly choir I do when I announce I jogged a mile in 9 minutes today when last week it was 11 minutes? Has the world become so callous that they can't even appreciate my words of knowledge regarding oat bran?

Not only do we seem boring when we talk endlessly about our new life of health, but sometimes we can become a self-styled trumpeter for the stomachs of the world. It's true, we're healthy and strong and we've got it together. People need only look at us to see that. We're free from the bondage of unhealthy eating, and our muscles are smiling at life. Why? It's *obvious.* We have the answers to the ails of the world. Here's a word of advice: Restrain yourself from giving the evil eye to your friend's sloppy hamburger. Hold back when you feel the urge to rush to the soapbox to preach against the sins of sodium at your next Cinco de Mayo fiesta. There will not be one person close to you who won't be influenced by *The All-New Free to Be Thin* lifestyle plan you've chosen. My friends, family, and acquaintances have changed their eating habits, not because of what I have *said,* but because of the *lifestyle* they have observed. Neva beams with pride at her grandchildren who are being offered fresh fruit, carrot sticks, and raw broccoli and cauliflower instead of sugary and fat-laden treats. The influence of *The All-New Free to Be Thin* lifestyle plan reaches even to the next generation!

The people in your world will observe a happier, more buoyant you when you become healthier. There truly is more to being thin than being thin. There's freedom, self-control, and strength.

The only way to share the love and goodness of the Lord is to do it in love. Jesus doesn't throw poisoned darts at sick people. He says, "Come to *me,* all you who are weary and burdened, and I will give you rest" (Matthew 11:28). He doesn't condemn people who are hurting and eating wrong foods for wrong motives. He says in love and mercy, "I am the bread of life!"

Eating healthy foods shouldn't become legalistic. Of primary importance always is Christ crucified, risen, and coming again. He came to set us free, and we must take care not to tie ourselves into knots over the evils of unhealthy food in the world. "Be *wise* as serpents, *harmless* as doves," He tells us.

Love is something you *do.* You do act kindly. You do encourage others. You do give your time and energy to help someone else. You do act as though other people's bodies are as important as yours.

The All-New Free to Be Thin lifestyle plan teaches us to be merciful with an understanding heart toward ourselves, and that makes us more understanding toward others. We are loving because we have become whole—spirit, soul, and body.

This is who you are. This is the kind of person you are:

You are a person of strength and compassion.

You have chosen a lifestyle of health and vitality.

You have chosen to be wise in your life's choices.

You have chosen self-understanding and awareness of your problems.

You have chosen not to run away from problems or to hurt yourself by overeating when you are hurting inside.

You are a person who has chosen exercise as a vital part of each day.

You care about yourself and other people.

You don't find fault and condemn people who are still eating junk food and hurting their body by lack of exercise.

You have mercy and compassion, and you earnestly pray for health and guidance for them.

You are precious to God.

You are an overcomer. You are free.

Free at last!

THE PROGRAM

SIMPLE, EASY, AND GREAT TIPS

Water. Drink water. We can't say it enough.

Teas and coffees. Some people think tea is healthier to drink than coffee. Actually, commercial tea contains caffeine, too, just as coffee does. It also has tannic acid in it, which is harmful to your health. Another deception is that decaffeinated coffee is better for you than regular coffee. The National Cancer Institute announced that the chemical *trichloroethylene,* or *TCE,* used in making decaffeinated coffee causes cancer in the livers of mice. It served a warning of a possible cancer danger to humans.

Instant tea. This tea contains malto dextrin, citric acid, artificial color and flavor, vegetable oil, and BHA (a preservative). Ouch!

Herb teas. Drink herb teas instead of orange pekoe or regular tea. There are dozens to choose from and you'll enjoy them. Carry a packet of herb tea bags in your pocket or purse for quick hot drinks when you are away from home or make ice tea at home. Delicious!

Hot chocolate and cocoa. Chocolate and cocoa contain caffeine from the cocoa bean. "Dutch" cocoa doesn't mean it comes from Holland; it means it's treated with alkali. Prepared cocoa mixes are loaded with unwanted additives. *Cara-Coa* is a good substitute. It's made of carob and contains no caffeine.

The food scares. You are not bound to a list of *never eat these.* You're free to eat the foods you know to be good for your body. As Christians we must not allow fear to have any part of our lives. This includes the area of food. We choose to *bless* our bodies at all times. Fear never motivates us; love does. We aren't afraid of the food we eat; we're in *control* of it.

Your budget. Be easy on your budget. You can afford healthy eating. Actually, it is easier on the budget to shop wisely for

213

healthy foods than grabbing the fast-food convenience stuff from the shelves and freezer. A bag of apples costs no more than a half gallon of ice cream. Frozen sugarless fruit juices cost no more than the six-packs of sugary soda pop you've been buying. Fresh fruit and natural foods are actually less expensive when you consider the price of potato chips, commercial chip dips, packaged cakes, Jell-O, and other junk foods. You'll be saving on your food bills when you eat healthy, natural foods. It's a fact.

Sharing foods. Some foods are share foods. An avocado is such a food. It is meant to be shared because one person shouldn't eat all those 375 calories alone. Baked goods prepared with all natural ingredients, including unrefined whole wheat flour and honey, safflower oil, nuts, dried unsulphured fruits, and eggs, are meant to be shared. Food so delicious and nutritious should be shared.

Leftovers. Never eat the leftovers after a meal. You need them less than the garbage disposal does. Sometimes it's wise to throw remaining food away rather than store it in the refrigerator. It may sound wasteful in this day of ecology, but those little dabs of this and that in your refrigerator will somehow find their way to your stomach if you don't get rid of them.

Kiddie food. Get rid of the kiddie food you've been addicted to. Ever notice how overeaters still eat the food little children are attracted to? Twinkies, cupcakes, ice cream, pizza, soda pop, macaroni and cheese, hot dogs, candy, mashed potatoes, french fries, hamburgers—ugh! If you are an adult, your tastes should have changed somewhat by now. A slightly different version of 1 Corinthians 13:11 could read, "When I was a child I ate as a child. But now I am an adult. I choose to eat wisely with nutrition and health in mind." *Now that I'm a grown-up person I put away childish foods!* Bless your heart (liver, lungs, bones, brain, muscles, and blood, too) as you chuck the old, fattening junk for the new, beautiful, healthy array of food for your body that God gave to you—healthy, natural foods.

Measuring foods. Be sure to measure foods, but don't panic. You won't have to carry around a scale and a set of measuring cups in your back pocket. You need to get acquainted with what half a cup of something looks like, though. It's important that you know how much a cup is or how a quarter of a cup of something looks. That's why you have to measure. If 1½ ounces of parmesan cheese has 170 calories, you'll need to know what it *looks* like before you can count it. One woman was shocked when she saw what half a cup of peas looked like on her plate. *You must measure your food for at least three weeks.* In three weeks' time you should know what certain measurements look like. Keep your scale and cups handy to check periodically after that.

Steaming food. A delicious way to serve vegetables is to steam them. Buy a steamer to set in your pan, add approximately an inch of water to the bottom of the pan and you'll have delicious, crisp, and tasty vegetables. You don't even need to add butter.

Stir fry. Using water instead of oil. There are many woks on the market, some electric. We love our woks and use them almost daily.

Thinking raw. Think raw. Be prepared for the "Wild Munchies." When you're suddenly seized with an uncontrollable urge to munch (and munch and munch), you should have fresh vegetables all sliced and waiting in a nice container in the refrigerator.

Canned foods. Some canned foods are fine. Canned foods are great to have on hand as long as they are not loaded with saturated fats and sodium. Excellent for cooking and as additions to any recipe are these: green chilies, pimentos, hearts of palm, water chestnuts, artichoke hearts, and mushrooms. Before using, be sure to rinse them to remove the salt. Look for canned tomatoes, tomato sauce, puree, and paste with low sodium. Garbanzo beans, green or waxed beans, beets without salt or sweeteners are good for many dishes. If you have a hard time finding low-sodium canned foods, rinse them in a colander or strainer to wash away the excess salt.

EXCHANGEABLE FOODS

Exchangeable foods are foods grouped together on a list because they are alike. Every food on the following list has about the same amount of carbohydrate, protein, fat, and calories. In the amount we have given here, all of the choices on each list are equal in their values. You can exchange any food on a list or trade it for any other food on the same list. Vary your diet.

We recommend and use exchanges because it is an easy, useful way to guarantee nutritional balance and maintain a chosen caloric intake without requiring detailed record keeping of counting individual calories.

EXCHANGES

DAIRY EXCHANGES

Each portion contains approximately 90 calories and is 1 percent fat or less by weight (15 percent of calories, or less, from fat).

Nonfat milk	8 oz.	Dry-curd cottage cheese	
Nonfat buttermilk	8 oz.	or hoop cheese	2 oz.
Nonfat yogurt	6 oz.	1% or less low-fat cottage cheese	2 oz.
Evaporated nonfat milk	4 oz.	Nonfat powdered milk	1/3 cup

VEGETABLE EXCHANGES

Each portion equals 1 cup of raw or 1 1/2 cup of cooked vegetables, and provides approximately 25 calories. This is not meant to be a complete list, and some other vegetables not listed here will be found listed with the Complex Carbohydrate Exchanges.

Artichoke, whole, base and ends of leaves (1 small)	Chilies	Mushrooms	Tomato (1 medium)
	Chinese cabbage	Okra	Tomatoes, canned in juice, unsalted
	Chives	Onions, all types	
	Coriander (cilantro)	Parsley	Tomato juice, unsalted (2/3 cup)
Asparagus	Cucumber	Pea pods, Chinese	
Beans, green or yellow	Eggplant	Peppers, red and green	
	Endive		Tomato paste, unsalted (3 Tbsp.)
Beets	Escarole	Pimento	
Bok choy	Greens: beet, collard, chard	Radishes	
Broccoli		Romaine lettuce	Tomato sauce, unsalted
Brussels sprouts	Jerusalem artichokes	Rhubarb*	
Cabbage		Rutabagas	Vegetable juice, unsalted (2/3 cup)
Carrots (1 medium)	Jicama	Shallots	
Cauliflower	Kale	Spinach*	
Celery	Leeks	Sprouts, assorted	Water chestnuts (4 medium)
Celery root	Lettuce	Squash:	
Cilantro	Lima beans, baby (1/4 cup)	zucchini,	Watercress
Chayote		spaghetti,	
Chicory	Mint	summer	

---

*High oxalic acid content. Not a good source of calcium.

HIGH-PROTEIN EXCHANGES

Each portion provides approximately 35 to 55 calories per ounce. High-protein exchanges are controlled because of their fat and cholesterol content. Although soybeans and tofu do not contain any cholesterol, they are higher in fat than any other legumes; 40 to 55 percent of their calories come from fat. You may select soybeans or tofu in place of fish, fowl, or meat on the Pritikin Lifetime Eating Plan.

In the chart below, note the total fat, cholesterol, and calorie contents, as well as the percentage of calories from fat, in 3½ ounce cooked servings of the foods. (Shrimp, which appears between the solid and dotted lines, is recommended in 2-ounce portions. Foods that appear below the dotted line are not recommended.)

Meat or Fish Source (3½ ounces cooked)	Fat (g)	Cholesterol (mg)	Calories
Abalone	0.3	54	49
Lobster, northern	.6	72	98
Pike	.9	50	113
Flounder	1.0	46	129
Cod, Atlantic	.9	55	105
Haddock	.9	74	112
Sole	.8	42	68
Scallops	1.4	52	112
Clams	2.0	67	148
Red Snapper, mixed species	1.7	47	128
Crab, Alaskan king	1.5	53	97
Tuna, white, water-packed	2.5	42	136
Turkey, white meat	3.2	69	157
Sea bass	2.6	53	124
Halibut	2.9	41	140
Chicken, white meat	3.6	85	165
Oysters	2.2	50	90
Trout	4.3	74	151
Beef, top round	5.4	84	184
Pork tenderloin, lean only	4.8	93	166
Swordfish	5.1	50	155
Beef, flank, lean only	7.3	90	195
Lamb, lean leg	7.0	93	184
Salmon, sockeye	11.0	87	216
Sardines, Pacific, water-packed, unsalted	12.0	81	178
Shrimp	1.1	133	99
Crayfish	1.4	178	114
Chicken, dark, without skin	9.7	93	205
T-bone steak, lean	10.4	80	214
Veal, rump and round	11.2	101	215
Turkey, dark without skin	11.5	89	221
Pork loin, top	14.9	94	258
Beef, lean ground, broiled	17.6	101	280
Beef, chuck (pot roast) fat and lean	24.4	99	337

YOUR BASIC MAINTENANCE FOOD GUIDE

FOOD GROUP	SUGGESTED DAILY SERVINGS	SERVING SIZES
Breads, cereals, and other grain products Whole grain or enriched	6–8	1 slice bread 1 oz. ready-to-eat cereal ½ c. cooked cereal ½ c. pasta, rice, or grits
Fruit Citrus, melons, berries, all other fruit	3–4	Whole piece of fruit ½ c. juice ¼ melon or ½ grapefruit ¼ c. dried fruit
Vegetables Dark green leafy, deep yellow, starchy, all other vegetables	4–6	½ c. cooked or chopped raw vegetable 1 c. raw vegetable
Meat, poultry, fish and shellfish Egg whites, yolks (limit yolks to 4 per week) Dried beans and peas (kidney, pink, lima, black, navy, etc.)	2–3 (A daily total of about 6 ounces)	2–3 oz. cooked lean meat, fish or poultry 2 eggs, 4 egg whites 1 c. cooked dried beans or peas
No-fat milk, cheese, yogurt	Teens: 3–4 Women up to 25: 3–4 Women over 25: 2–3 Men: 2–3	1 c. skim milk 1 c. low-fat yogurt 1½ oz. low-fat cheese
Fats (unsaturated) Vegetable oils, salad dressings, spreads, nuts	Women: 3–6 Men: 4–9	1 tsp. spreads and vegetable oils 1 Tbsp. salad dressing 1 oz. nuts

Daily Requirements	Women	Men
Fat	20–40 grams	30–60 grams
Fiber	20–40 grams	up to 50 grams
Protein	44 grams	56 grams
Sodium	1 gram (1,000 milligrams)	1 gram (1,000 milligrams)

FRUIT EXCHANGES

Fresh, dried, frozen, or canned fruit, without sugar or syrup. Each portion provides approximately 60 calories.

Fruit	Portion	Fruit	Portion
Apple	1 small (2" diam.)	Lime juice	½ cup
Apple juice or cider	⅓ cup	Loquats	13
Applesauce, unsweetened	½ cup	Mandarin oranges	¾ cup
Apricots, fresh	4 medium	Mango	½ small
Apricots, dried	7 halves	Nectarine	1 (1½" diam.)
Banana	½ medium	Orange	1 (2½" diam.)
Berries: boysenberries, raspberries,		Orange juice	½ cup
blueberries	¾	Papaya	1 cup
Cantaloupe	⅓ (5" diam.)	Passion fruit	1
Cherries	12 large	Passion fruit juice	⅓ cup
Cranberries, unsweetened	1 cup	Peach	1 (2¾" diam.)
Crenshaw melon	2" wedge	Pear	1 small
Dates	2½ medium	Persimmon, native	2 medium
Date sugar	1 Tbsp.	Pineapple, fresh	¾ cup
Figs, fresh	2 (2" diam.)	Pineapple, canned without sugar	⅓ cup
Figs, dried	1½	Pineapple juice	½ cup
Fruit cocktail	½ cup	Plantain	½ small
Fruit juice concentrate	2 Tbsp. (1 oz.)	Plums	2 (2" diam.)
Grapefruit	½ medium	Pomegranate	½
Grapefruit juice	½ cup	Prunes, fresh	2 medium
Grapes	15 small	Prunes, dried	3
Grape juice	⅓ cup	Prune juice	⅓ cup
Guava	1½	Raisins	2 Tbsp.
Honeydew melon	⅛ medium	Strawberries	1¼ cup
Kiwi	1 large	Tangerines	2 (2½" diam.)
Kumquats	5	Watermelon	1¼ cup
Lemon juice	½ cup		

YOUR MARVELOUS METABOLISM

Exercise affects your metabolism, which is the combustion process that goes on in your cells when carbohydrates in the form of glucose or glycogen and oxygen are burned, creating energy. The energy released as this process is going on is measured in calories. That's why we say we "burn up calories." Your metabolic rate goes up when you exercise vigorously, and it takes more time to slow down again afterward. This means you actually continue to burn calories even after you stop exercising. The greater the ratio of lean tissue you have to body fat, the more calories you will burn. This is because lean tissue is more highly oxygenated than fat, and it keeps the metabolic process going longer. If you exercise long enough at one time, your muscles use fat for fuel instead of carbohydrates. Your endurance is increased because your muscles will program to store the carbohydrates instead of the fat.

Keep in mind that it takes the stomach *four hours* to empty an average meal. This means that snacking between meals add food to an already working stomach and increases the emptying time—sometimes to as much as *nine hours.* In addition, the fermentation created in the stomach can be harmful to your body, mind, and emotions. It is recommended that *five hours* be allowed to lapse between the end of one meal and the next time you eat.

If you're the kind of person who likes to nibble and snack all day instead of eating meals, it can be harmful to your body because of poor absorption of nutrients and the reduction of the amount of protein available for the body to use.

You can throw away that old excuse about having a very slow metabolism, and you can stop saying that everything you eat turns to fat. Your metabolism is a process of breaking down the food you eat. If you stop eating such heavy, fattening foods, your metabolism will be a lot happier. Yes, you may have slower metabolism now, but that *can* be changed.

BE "IN THE KNOW"

KNOW WHAT'S HAPPENING TO YOUR BODY

- Too much salt in your diet:
  Excessive sodium intake has been associated with high blood pressure and cardiovascular disease.
- Too much fat in your diet:
  High dietary fat, saturated fat, and cholesterol intakes influence risk factors to heart disease.
- Not enough fiber and vitamins:
  High dietary fat intake, and low vitamin A and fiber intakes have been associated with some cancers, primarily stomach, digestive, breast, and colon cancers.
- Not enough nutrition knowledge:

Inadequate nutrition may increase susceptibility to infections and/or impair the body's response to fight infections. Inadequate nutrition may be associated with poor pregnancy outcome, including low-birth-weight infants, and suboptimal mental and physical development of children.

KNOW HOW TO SWITCH FROM HIGH-FAT TO LOW-FAT

One of the most healthy decisions you'll ever make is to decrease fat and cholesterol in your diet. It's easy. Here are some substitutes that will reduce the amount of fat and cholesterol you eat. Consult this list often.

HIGH-FAT ITEM	LOW-FAT SUBSTITUTE
Mayonnaise, sour cream	Use nonfat yogurt mixed with a small amount of nonfat buttermilk or powdered nonfat milk. Add spices to use with fish, chicken, baked potatoes, pasta, shredded cabbage (for coleslaw), or fruit, seasoning appropriately for the dish. It's a great sandwich spread, too: Add finely chopped vegetables or fresh herbs like dill, parsley, dry or prepared mustard, chives, or scallions, alone or in combination, for extra flavor. Experiment!
1 whole egg	2 egg whites (avoid substitutes since these contain colorings and additives, among other artificial ingredients).
Cream, Half-and-Half	Evaporated skim milk (or powdered nonfat milk) adds a creamy texture to sauces and soups.
Fatty meats	Round or flank steak; white-meat chicken or turkey (skinless); seafood.
Oil and fat in cooking	Cook with defatted low-sodium chicken or beef broth, vinegar, lemon juice, or water; nonstick cookware. No-stick sprays do contain some oil.
Butter, margarine	Apple butter, no-added-sugar fruit spreads and jams, fresh fruit puree.

KNOW THESE 18 WAYS TO CUT DOWN ON FAT

1. Read labels carefully.
   - identify differences between polyunsaturated and saturated oils
   - an unidentified vegetable fat, oil, or shortening on a label usually indicates palm or coconut oil
2. Choose leaner cuts of meat, and trim away visible fat.
   - instead of regular hamburger, buy ground round
   - choose turkey or chicken when possible
   - avoid processed luncheon meats (containing nitrates)
3. Stay away from pan-frying meats.
   - bake, broil, or roast instead
   - baste with tomato or lemon juice, broth or wine
4. Use non-stick skillets and baking pans.
   - avoid unnecessary greasing
5. Serve smaller portions, or portions with a lower meat content.
   - serve soups and stews with more vegetables and whole-grain breads
6. Avoid red meats, stick to chicken, turkey, or fish.
   - fish and poultry—without skin—are low in saturated fat and cholesterol
   - think of meat as an accent to your meal, not the main feature
7. Avoid pre-breaded foods and commercial coating mixes.
   - chicken coated with plain bread crumbs and herbs are lower in saturated fats
   - coconut oil and palm oil are in high concentration in commercial mixes
8. When cooking sauces, brown the meat separately and drain the fat before adding other ingredients.
   - chilling after draining will allow you to remove additional fat
9. Start using margarine instead of butter.
   - choose a margarine that has a high ratio of polyunsaturated to saturated fats
   - safflower, sunflower, and corn oil are good choices and high in polyunsaturates
   - margarine that lists liquid oils or water as the first ingredient are best
10. Choose low-fat milk instead of whole milk.

- skim milk, low-fat milk, and nonfat dry milk offer a triple treat—less saturated fats, cholesterol, and calories

11. Switch to low-fat cheeses.
    - cream cheese and cheddar cheese have a high fat content
    - look for cottage cheese, mozzarella, riccota, Swiss, and other cheeses made with skim or part skim milk

12. Instead of ice cream, eat low-fat frozen yogurt, ice milk, or frozen fruit bars.
    - these foods may be high in calories but they are low in fat

13. Avoid non-dairy creamers and whipped toppings.
    - use low-fat milk or nonfat dried milk for creamers
    - use yogurt or fruit for toppings

14. Reduce egg yolks.
    - egg yolks have the highest concentration of cholesterol; use 2 egg whites for one egg

15. In cooking and baking, experiment with ingredients.
    - fats and oils usually can be reduced without changing taste and texture
    - use 2 egg whites in place of one egg with yolk

16. Watch the salad dressings.
    - dressings like blue cheese and creamy Italian are high in fat
    - for creamy dressings use low-fat yogurt and cottage cheese

17. Avoid commercial baked goods, frostings, and mixes.
    - select a mix that lets *you* add a healthy type of oil

18. Whenever possible, stay away from frozen meals, TV dinners, packaged and canned foods.

Sources: Select Committee on Nutrition and Human Needs, United States Senate, Dietary Goals for the United States, second edition, 1977, U.S. Government Printing Office, Washington, D.C.

The New Pritikin Program